POLISH FOLKLORE

AND

MYTH

POLISH FOLKLORE AND MYTH

Collected and edited by Joanne Asala
Wycinanki designs by Alice Wadowski-Bak

Penfield BOOKS

Dedications

To my grandmother, Emma Kuyat Dawson, who taught me to take pride in my Polish heritage by sharing her stories and memories of growing up.

— Joanne Asala

Wycinanki dedicated to my son Kenneth Michael Bak for his continuous inspiration.

— Alice Wadowski-Bak

Editors: Joan Liffring-Zug Bourret, Dorothy Crum and Melinda Bradnan
Graphic design: Deborah Walkoczy

ISBN-13: 978-1572160897

About the Author

Joanne Asala is the editor of more than thirty books on traditional folktales, customs, and cooking, including *Polish Proverbs, Czech Proverbs,* and *Fairy Tales of the Slav Peasants and Herdsmen.* Asala, a graduate of the University of Iowa with an emphasis on Medieval English literature, has traveled extensively throughout Eastern and Western Europe in order to collect folklore material firsthand. Her most recent adventure was a summer spent backpacking through the islands in the North Atlantic in order to gather information on Viking customs. Of Polish and Finnish descent, she fondly remembers her grandmother, Emma Kuyat Dawson, telling her stories of life in Chicago's Polish neighborhood. Currently, Ms. Asala divides her time between Chicago, Illinois, and Irvine, Scotland.

About the Artist

Alice Wadowski-Bak's wycinanki also highlights *Polish Proverbs,* another Penfield Press publication by Joanne Asala. Alice works in a variety of media that includes the painting, *History of the Saints in the Americas,* a commissioned work for Pope John Paul II, which was sponsored by the Blue Army Organization based in New Jersey.

Her artwork, including watercolors, etchings, acrylics and pen-and-ink drawings, can be found worldwide in numerous private collections and galleries. Working for a number of years from her studio in New York City, she has illustrated magazines and books, as well as designed textiles.

Alice studied at Syracuse University; graduated from the University of Buffalo with a Bachelor of Fine Arts degree, and earned her Master's degree from Niagara University. A native of Niagara Falls, New York, she says her greatest achievement is her two grown sons Kenneth and Gregory (who is married to Rebecca, a professional harpist). Alice is now the proud grandmother of Natalie Grace.

Table of Contents

The Art of Wycinanki

Wycinanki — paper cutting for decoration — began to appear in Poland in the middle of the 1800s, especially in the rural areas. The people used the supplies at hand to create spontaneous folk art, and sheep shears were found in most farm homes. The designs achieved by cutting paper traditionally decorate cottage walls, rafters, cupboards and windows, especially at Easter and Christmastime. Springtime might be reflected with images of birds, trees, and flowers. Created as they are cut, the designs exude a fresh non-labored appeal. Paper may be folded, layered, colored, overlaid or in a variety of combinations to create whimsical and stunning art work.

The technique is related to the ancient Chinese art of using a sharp knife to create a stencil type, block print image.

Alice Wadowski-Bak, paper-cut artist, explores both the positive and negative images of wycinanki as well as oriental stencil cutting.

The Terrible *Wilas*

The Wilas *(sometimes known as* Rusalkas*) are feminine spirits who live in the mountains, woods, and waterways of Poland. Some tribes say that they are very beautiful, while others believe the* Wilas *are ugly, vicious, and bent on destruction. Almost all agree that they are the souls of dead maidens who delight in leading shepherds and young boys astray. Peasants once placed flowers and offerings of sweets at the entrances of caves believed to be the dwelling spots of the terrible* Wilas.

There was once a poor orphan named Baltazar. As he had neither father nor mother he was forced to go out into the world to earn a living. He traveled a long way, through city and town, through hill and valley, and through field and forest. He was hungry, and he was tired, and he was very, very worried that he would never find honest work. Who would vouch for a homeless boy?

After a while, Baltazar came to a tiny cabin in the woods. In the doorway sat a very old man, smoking a pipe. A worn and tattered scarf covered his eyes. There were half-a-dozen goats bleating from the shed, and the old man called out to them, "Hush, my darlings. I would take you to pasture if I could, but I am a poor blind man. The hired boy ran off and there is no one to tend you."

"Let me watch them, Grandfather," said Baltazar. "I will pasture your goats. What's more, I can take care of you."

"Who's there?" asked the old man, cocking his head to one side.

"Baltazar, Sir. Hire me on, and I'll tend to your chores."

"Well now, isn't this well timed?" cackled the old man. "Sure, I'll hire you on. Drive the goats to the high pasture, but don't let them climb too high up the hill. The *Wilas* will come upon you and gobble up your eyes, just as they have eaten mine." He pulled the rag aside, and where his eyes should have been were two empty sockets.

It took Baltazar a moment to find his voice, but he managed to say bravely, "Never fear, Grandfather, the *Wilas* won't get my eyes!"

"That's the spirit, my boy! When you come back, you can fix us both a bit of supper."

Baltazar led the goats from the stall and followed them up to the high pasture. For several days he followed the old man's instructions, but on the morning of the third day he chanced to look up the hill. "The grass up there looks green and fresh," he mused. "The goats can eat their fill, and gladly. Why should I be afraid of the *Wilas?* They're nothing but a *bajka,* a fairy tale."

None-the-less, Baltazar rose and broke off three green shoots of bramble and put them in his hat as a protection against evil. Then he drove the goats straight up the path. The goats kicked up their heels and settled to grazing in the fresh grass. The orphan lad sat down in the shade to rest and take a nap.

He was not dozing for long when all of a sudden — and he wasn't quite sure how she could have arrived without his hearing her — there stood before him a maiden with raven-black hair, rosy cheeks and two eyes like ripe sloes. She was dressed all in white, with white flowers entwined in her hair. "Bless you, young goatherd," she laughed.

"And you as well," he replied shakily.

"I've brought you a gift," she smiled.

"A gift?"

"Yes. It's an apple from our garden, very delicious and sweet. I'll give you one, so that you may know how good you are." She pulled from her sleeve an apple as rosy as her complexion. "Take it with my regards."

Fear gripped the young orphan's heart, but he did not show it. He knew that this wonderful creature was a *Wila,* and that the apple would no doubt put him to sleep so that she could tear out and devour his eyes.

"Thank you," he said, trying to smile in return. "You're very kind, but my master has an apple tree near the shed with apples that are finer still. I have eaten enough and more."

"If you'd rather not...." the maiden shrugged, and without a backward glance she wandered further up the path.

"That was close," thought Baltazar. "There will be no napping today."

But just as his eyelids were beginning to droop, a second maiden, more beautiful than the first, appeared out of nowhere.

"Good day to you, Goatherd," she smiled. "I have a gift for you."

"A gift?" asked Baltazar.

"Oh yes, I've brought you a rose." From behind her back she brought forth a rose. It was the most perfect rose that the young orphan had ever seen. "I've just plucked it off our rosebush," the maiden continued, "and I thought you'd like to have it. It smells very nice. Here, smell it for yourself."

Baltazar ignored the rose the maiden held out to him. He knew that to touch it would spell his doom. "My master has a rosebush near the house," he said, "on it are roses that would make this one wilt in comparison."

"Well I never...." the maiden growled, storming out of the pasture.

Almost immediately a third beauty came along. She was more beautiful than either of her sisters. "Hello, Baltazar," she said. "You're a fine-looking lad, but you'd be finer still if you took a brush to your hair. Come, let me comb it for you."

Baltazar could think of nothing to say in return, and so sat quietly as the maiden approached. Then he remembered his hat! He removed it from his head, drew out a bramble shoot, and whack! He struck the comb from the girl's hands. She screamed, "Help, my sisters! Come quickly!" She tried to run away, but found her feet rooted to the spot. Bramble has that kind of power.

"That's enough of that," said Baltazar, tying her hands together with the bramble. Just then the other maidens returned to the clearing.

"Release her at once," said the first of them.

"Release her yourself," said Baltazar.

"We cannot," said the second maiden. "See how tender our hands are? We'll be sure to prick ourselves on the brambles." Before they could say another word, Baltazar leaped forward and whack! whack! He struck them each with the remaining bramble shoots and bound their hands securely.

"I've got you now!" said the goatherd. "And it's here you'll stay until I get back."

Baltazar went down the hill to get the old man. "Come, Grandfather," he said. "I've found somebody who can help you see again."

The young orphan led the old man back up the hill to where the sisters waited, unable to run away as long as the bramble held them. "Now tell me where the old man's eyes are," he said to the first maiden, "or I'll throw you over the cliff and into the river below."

The *Wila* wept, "I don't know what you're talking about!" she wailed. "I don't have his eyes!" But as Baltazar went to pick her up, she screamed, "Don't, please don't! Release me, and I'll take you to where we keep the eyes."

She led him to a cavern up the hill. Inside was a pile of eyes: brown eyes, blue eyes, black and green. She drew out a pair of tawny gold eyes and handed them to Baltazar. "Here," she said, "these are the old man's eyes."

But when Baltazar placed them in the old man's sockets, the poor man began to cry, "Oh, no! These aren't my eyes at all. These once belonged to an owl!"

Baltazar picked up the maiden, ignoring her protests, and tossed her without ceremony into the water below. Then he turned to the second *Wila*. "Will you tell me which eyes belong to the old man?"

"Of course," she nodded, "I'll take you to the cavern." She rummaged around in the pile of eyes and finally drew out two silvery grey orbs.

"Are you sure these are the right pair?" asked Baltazar.

"Yes," she nodded. "Pop them in. He'll see just as well as before."

"Oh no!" cried the old man as he glanced around the cavern with his new eyes. "These aren't mine at all. They once belonged to a wolf!"

"You had your chance," said Baltazar. He picked up the *Wila* and tossed her into the river below.

"Now," he said to the youngest of the *Wilas,* "you will tell me where the old man's eyes are, or suffer the same fate as your sisters."

"I will," she nodded, and led old man and boy back to the cavern.

"What color were your eyes?" Baltazar asked the old man. "We'll not be fooled again."

"As I recall, they were brown," said his companion.

"You heard him, Witch," said Baltazar. "His eyes were brown."

And so the *Wila* dug through the pile for a very long time, finally bringing out a pair of brown eyes.

"Ah, that's better," said the boy. "These are definitely the proper pair."

But when he inserted them, the old man cried out again that these weren't his eyes. "These once belonged to a bear!" he groaned. "They're not mine at all."

Baltazar knew he was being cheated and said, "You had your chance, and you will follow your sisters." He picked her up and tossed her over the cliff.

"Now what will we do?" asked the old man miserably.

"We will try each pair until we find the right set," Baltazar sighed. "It shouldn't take long." At last, at the bottom of the pile, the goatherd found the old man's eyes.

"Ah!" cried the old man. "These are mine. Now I can see again!"

Afterwards Baltazar and the old man returned to the cabin in the woods where they lived for many a year. Baltazar tended the goats while the old man cooked and cleaned, and both were quite happy. Nor were they ever again troubled by the *Wilas*.

The Violin

In Slavic countries there is a curse which still states, "May the black god devour you!" It hearkens to a time when many Slavs believed in two gods: Byelobog *the white god and* Chernobog *the black god, classic examples of good and evil. Many of today's folktales of the devil are perhaps old, old tales of* Chernobog.

Garek could play the violin, and he could play very well. He was always in demand for dances and birthday celebrations, and he was the first to be called to play at funerals and wakes. He loved to play the violin, and grew quite rich by doing so. "I'd be the happiest man alive if it weren't for one thing," he told his wife one evening.

"And what is that, my love?" she asked, looking up from her sewing.

"I'm afraid of growing old. What will happen to my music when my hands become bent and twisted with age?"

It was a problem that kept him awake most nights. One evening, when he again couldn't sleep, he wandered out onto the porch. There he found a strange old man sitting quite comfortably in the rocker, as if he owned the chair and the homestead.

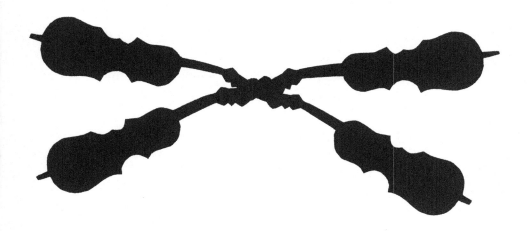

"Who the devil are you?" demanded Garek.

"You got it in one try!" laughed the stranger. "I am the devil."

"And what do you want?" asked Garek. "I'm a God-fearing man and I go to church. You have no claim on me."

"I've come to make a deal. I'll give you eternal youth if you give me your soul."

"Are you trying to trick me?" asked Garek suspiciously. "If I'm to remain a young man forever, how am I to die? If I don't die, how will you collect my soul?"

"A clever man!" laughed the devil. "I'll put this condition on the deal. You shall remain young and hearty until the end of time as long as you never set foot in Rome."

"That should be easy enough to avoid," nodded Garek. "The Holy City is a great many leagues away."

The devil only smiled and waved farewell before disappearing in a haze of smoke.

"Now that was quite the bargain," thought Garek. "I'm sure to come out ahead."

The very next morning he packed his bag and his violin and hit the open road. It was his plan to seek even greater fame and fortune with his music. By nightfall he reached a village where no one knew his name. He stopped at the first tavern he saw and ordered a pint of beer. As he took his first sip, he was suddenly seized with a pain in his chest and collapsed to the floor. The barkeep came out from behind the counter to offer what aid he could, but it was too late. Garek lay dying. "I…I don't understand…." he gasped. "What is this place?"

"Rome," said the barkeep. "An odd name, surely, but one my father gave me after he made a pilgrimage to the Holy City. I named the bar after myself."

The foolish young man died, and his soul was given up to the devil. And as for the violin? It hangs on a wall at the tavern still. On the anniversary of the musician's death, some say, the violin will break out in a mournful dirge for the death of its ill-fated owner.

The Headache Cure

According to ancient Polish myth, the dog is a symbol of the Great Mother Goddess worshiped before the coming of Christianity. Later Slavic myth makes the dog an enemy of both vampires and snakes.

Once upon a time when animals could talk, Michalek the dog was stricken with a headache. If you've ever had a headache, then you know how he must have felt. The pain nearly drove him mad. He ran back and forth, shaking his head and howling his agony, unable to do anything to stop his head from pounding. As he was running past the cow pasture, he nearly stepped on a coiled snake warming herself in the sun.

"Whoa there, friend dog," hissed Sabinka. "You've nearly trampled me into the earth. What is it that has you running like a mad dog?"

"I'm sorry!" wailed Michalek. "But the ache in my head is such that I hardly know where I'm going. My head is likely to split in two and I can't seem to do a thing about it."

"I should have guessed," nodded Sabinka wisely. "If you want my advice, I know a cure. I have a headache myself, but the only cure I know is for dogs. It won't help a snake at all."

"I'll try anything!" moaned the dog. "Just tell me quickly."

"Climb through the fence into the cow pasture," said the snake, "and fill your belly with grass. Your headache will disappear in no time; pasture grass has that kind of power."

Michalek did as the snake instructed, and soon his headache was gone.

"Better than ever, I see," smiled the snake. "I'm glad I could be of help to you."

Michalek, feeling much better, looked down at the snake and frowned. He was not happy to have such a creature prove to be his better. What would the other dogs think? Where he should have felt gratitude, Michalek felt only spite. He decided to pay back the snake's good deed with evil intentions.

"You've helped me, surely," said the dog, smiling as best he could, "and now it's my turn to help you. I may not know how to cure my own headaches, but I do know a cure for a snake's headache that works better than any *czarownica's** charm. I learned it from a snake near the village of Yegorevsk, when my master and I were traveling."

"Really?" asked Sabinka hopefully. "I'd be forever obliged to you."

"It's quite simple, really," said Michalek the dog. "All you need to do is stretch yourself across the road. The pain in your head will be gone in no time!"

"Now why didn't I think of that!" remarked the snake. "It was good fortune, indeed, that we met on this road."

"Indeed," laughed the dog to himself.

Sabinka did as the dog suggested, and stetched out in the road beside the pasture. It was not long before a peasant came down the road carrying a stout walking stick. When he came across the poor snake, he took no chances and struck her quickly across the head. It was over in an instant. Poor Sabinka! But the dog spoke true — the snake no longer felt any pain. Michalek's headache cure worked. Ever since that day, when a snake has a headache it will stretch itself out in the road. If it escapes unhurt, the headache will disappear; if its head is crushed, all its worries are over. Yes, Michalek's cure proved true. But ever since that time, dogs and snakes have been mortal enemies.

czarownica – enchantress or witch

The Death Shroud

Many pagan customs have lasted into Christian times, such as the funeral feast often held in the cemetery. The feast is a remnant of the trizna, *a meal dedicated to the spirit of the deceased.*

There was once a woman of the village of Kuyat who had a tiny daughter named Joasia. She had long red curls that bounced and shone like sunset on the water, and eyes as green as the forest depths. All who looked upon the tiny child could not help but fall in love with her. "She's bound for greatness," boasted her mother. "As sure as I stand here, a prince will one day come and take her from our humble home."

The mother should have known better! One should not speak such wishful praises aloud for fear of catching the jealous eye of the *Zorya*, a sister of fate.

One bright spring morning, shortly after her sixth birthday, the auburn-haired girl fell sick and died. She was buried in the church cemetery and everyone in the village came to pay their respects. Afterwards a feast, with bread and meat and lots of strong beer, was held right in the cemetery. The village had not seen such a feast in many a year, and Joasia's mother should have been proud. Grief blinded the poor woman, however, and she could not be consoled. Both day and night she wept for her darling daughter.

It was not long afterwards that Joasia appeared to her mother in the tiny house they had shared. "Do not cry, Mother," said the ghost sitting by the fire. "Your tears are breaking my heart. How can I sleep knowing you are in such pain?"

The mother crossed herself rapidly and tossed blessed water at the apparition, fearing it was really a *naw,* a demon spirit with the face of her beloved daughter. When the vision did not fade away, she too sat by the fire. "How can I not cry knowing you are in the cold ground?" she countered.

And because the poor woman would not stop her weeping, Joasia

appeared each night by the fire. "Mother," she'd beg, "please, stop. I can't bear to see you so unhappy."

Still the poor mother wept bitter tears.

On the seventh night Joasia returned, this time wrapped in her burial shroud. "Mother," she said, "cease with your tears. I cannot sleep in my grave for my shroud is never dry because of your tears which constantly soak it."

When the mother heard this, she was terribly afraid. "I do not wish to be the cause of your unrest," she said, wiping away the last of her tears. "Go to sleep, my child. I shall cry no more."

Joasia appeared to her mother one final time after that, holding in her hand a rose. "Look, Mother," said the pretty little spirit, "my shroud is quite dry, and I can go to my final rest. This flower, plucked from the gardens of paradise, is for you."

And so the mother bowed to the will of heaven and suffered her sadness in silence. As for the flower? It can be seen on the altar of the village church, a testament to the world beyond. Go and look for yourself, it is there still.

Marya and the *Rusaje*

The linden, or lime blossom, was once sacred to the Poles. Like the rowan, it is thought to protect against lightning and evil spirits. People sometimes still leave offerings tied to the branches of a linden tree, perhaps in remembrance of an ancient custom or pagan belief.

Once upon a time, there lived a rich man named Bartos who lived with his wife Nadzia and his lovely daughter Marya. Nadzia was a kind, sweet woman, and her husband loved her very dearly. Although he would have given his life to save her, he could do nothing when she fell sick and lay dying.

"My daughter," said Nadzia from her death bed. "Come closer."

"Yes, Mother?" said Marya, wiping her mother's brow with a cool rag. "What is it?"

"I am to die very soon, my daughter, and I want you to promise me something. Promise me, that when the time comes, you will plant a linden tree on my grave so that the birds can find food and shelter."

It was a bitterly cold day in winter when Nadzia passed away, and a beautiful spring morning when Bartos married again. His new wife was a widow woman with two daughters near Marya's age. "Here is something your mother and I were never able to give you," Bartos told his daughter, "sisters to love and cherish you."

Although they always acted sweet and kind in the presence of their stepfather, the girls did not care for their new sister Marya. They were envious of her shining hair and her fair complexion. They despised her for her tinkling laugh and her soft voice. And they hated her because Bartos seemed to love her best.

It was not long afterwards that Bartos was attacked by highwaymen and killed for his purse of gold coins. "Now you shall be our little-slave girl," the stepmother told Marya. "You shall do all of the cooking and cleaning while my daughters tend to their studies and their sewing."

"But this is my house too!" Marya protested.

"But I rule here now," said the stepmother. "And if you don't like it you can take to the road. There's none that will stop you."

Marya ran weeping to her room, and none came to comfort her. The day grew late and shadows lengthened in the room, and still the poor orphan girl sat crying on her windowsill.

"Stop your weeping this instant," said a voice from above.

"Who's there?" cried Marya, casting glances both right and left.

"Above you in the tree, foolish girl. Now stop your crying and tell me what has made you so sad."

Marya looked up to see a tiny magpie sitting in the tree by her window. "I am all alone in this world," she said. "My mother and my father are dead, and there is no one here to love me."

"Oh, my poor child! Why do you not go and complain to the linden tree? Ask for counsel, and perhaps your heavy heart will be lightened."

So Marya did just that. She wiped the tears from her eyes, combed her hair, and went down to her mother's grave. She knelt down beside the linden tree that she had planted and poured out all of her heartaches.

"In whom do you put your trust, my child?" says a voice from the tree, sounding for all the world like her dear mother.

"In God," she promptly replied.

"Well, my darling," said the tree, "put your trust in God and call to the cock and the hen. There's work you must do this evening that you cannot do alone."

"What work is that?" asked Marya. "There are no more chores this evening." But the tree spoke not another word.

Just then she heard her stepsisters calling for her. "Marya, Marya! Come here this instant you silly girl! The king has announced a dance for this evening and all the village maidens are to attend."

"Really?" asked Marya, seeing for once a chance at laughter and gaiety. "I know just the dress I'm going to wear."

"Who says you are to go?" said the first stepsister. "We need you to help us get ready."

Marya, being the sweet girl that she is, helped her sisters to dress.

"Now I can get dressed, too," she said. "It won't take but a moment."

"Your chores are not done, Marya," said her stepmother, casting a handful of lentils into the ashes from the fire. "First you must pick those lentils up. Then you can go."

When her stepmother and sisters left for the ball, Marya called for the hen and the cock. "I need your help," she said. "I cannot possibly separate all of these lentils by myself."

After the birds picked up every last lentil and placed them back in the bowl, the hen turned to the girl and said, "Go to the linden tree, and shake it hard."

When Marya had done so, a light appeared in the darkness and she saw a woman sitting on the summit of the tree. She was as tall as Marya and dressed in a shining gold gown. In her hands she held a basket and a gold wand.

"The *Rusaje*," Marya breathed. "I hardly dared hope...."

With a gentle smile the fairy queen took an egg from her basket and struck it with her wand. Instantly it turned into a handsome coach. Then she pulled six tiny mice from her basket and tapped each one on the head. These became six coal black horses to pull the coach. Finally she pulled out two multi-colored butterflies to become the footmen and a ladybug to become the coachman.

"But we must dress you better than this," said the fairy queen, and these were the first words she spoke to the awestruck girl. She waved her wand over Marya and her rags disappeared. She was dressed in a gown as fine as any that belonged to an empress, with ribbons and flowers entwined in her hair. "Now hurry, there is still plenty of time to dance with the prince," said the fairy. "But be sure to return home before the cock crows for the third time, or else everyone will discover our little secret."

Marya promised to obey the *Rusaje's* instructions and left for the ball, hardly daring to believe that such a miracle was hers.

Word quickly spread through the king's assembled guests that a maginifent princess was coming to the ball. The prince himself went out to meet Marya and took her by the elbow to lead her through the crowd. Immediately all fell silent, the violins were hushed, and the people parted to let the strange princess pass.

"Who is she?" someone whispered aloud what they were all thinking.

"More importantly, who designed her gown?" whispered another, and all the ladies present vowed to copy the pattern and cut of Marya's fine clothes, having never seen their equal.

The prince led Marya to a seat next to his own, and dinner was served. Marya found herself seated across from her own sisters, who did not recognize her. She even presented them with the oranges and the chocolates the prince gave her, which of course very much surprised them. "How fortunate for us to be so honored by this strange princess!" the sisters beamed at one another. "We are the talk of everyone here. And won't Marya be green with envy when we tell her of this!"

After dinner, the prince led Marya to the dance floor. He never left her side and never ceased with his compliments and words of love. They danced so gracefully together that it looked as if they had done nothing else with their lives but this. "A match made in heaven!" sighed many a mother, wishing that it was her own daughter the prince danced with.

Marya so enjoyed the attention that it was with some surprise that she heard the cock crow. "Oh dear!" she cried. "I must go!"

"What is it, my love?" asked the prince, while in the background the cock crowed a second time.

"I don't have time to explain!" she said, and ran from the room as nimble as any deer. The prince followed but he could not overtake her.

She left behind one of her embroidered slippers, which the prince picked up and held close to his heart.

Marya made it home, but not before the cock crowed a third time and the sun rose in the sky. Her coach was once again a hen's egg; her fine horses became tiny mice; her footmen spread their wings and flew away as butterflies, and her coachman, again a ladybug, scurried to hide in the wet leaves along the road. Marya looked down to see that her fine gown was gone and all that remained from the evening was the one lone shoe, the mate to the one she dropped. This she kept hidden in her pocket, and hurried home.

When her stepsisters arrived what a tale they had to tell! "You should have seen the foreign princess!" they said to Marya. "The prince only had eyes for her."

"What became of her?" asked Marya.

"She ran away suddenly when the cock began to crow. She left in such haste that all that remained of her visit was a tiny embroidered slipper, the prettiest little shoe in the world!"

"I wish I could have been there," sighed Marya.

"You? Ha! As if they would let a grubby little ash-maiden like you into the king's castle."

A few days later the king's son announced that he would marry the woman whose foot fit into the embroidered slipper. He sent his steward out to try the slipper on all the princesses in the neighborhood, then all of the great ladies, then all of the royal courts, but it was in vain. Not one of them could fit her foot into the elegant shoe.

Finally the prince decided to try it on the common ladies, and the steward came at last to the house of Marya. The stepsisters tried, but could not fit their large feet into the shoe.

"Let me try!" said Marya.

"You!" her sisters burst out laughing. "You weren't even there!"

"Oh, but I was," said Marya quietly. "Let me try on the slipper."

The steward looked Marya straight in the eyes and said, "Yes, I believe you were."

"But she's just our maid!" protested the stepmother. "How can you let her try on the shoe?"

"Nevertheless, I have my orders," said the steward. "Every maiden is to try on the shoe."

Of course, the shoe fit Marya perfectly, for it was made for her foot alone. Everyone there was astonished, to be sure, but not as surprised as they were when Marya pulled the other shoe from her pocket. "Here is its mate," she smiled sweetly.

Before her stepsisters could utter a single word of protest, the *Rusaje* came into the room and touched Marya on the forehead with her wand. A bright light filled the room, and when it faded Marya stood before them in a gown finer than the one she wore to the ball.

Her sisters threw themselves at her feet, begging her for forgiveness.

"By rights I should send you to the fireplace to separate lentils from ashes," she said severely, "but you are my sisters and I will forgive you." Then she took them to the castle where she married her prince, and all remained happy to the end of their days.

The Three Magic Wishes

Saule *is the pre-Christian sun goddess of the Slavic lands. Some legends say that her golden chariot is pulled by twin steeds, known as the* Asviniai, *while other stories tell of six great cats that lead their mistress across the sky. The following tale seems to be a folklore memory of an ancient belief system.*

There was once — I don't know where, at the other side of seven times seven countries or even beyond them — a poor man who was married to a very pretty young wife. They loved each other dearly and had only one real complaint: neither of them had more than a coin or two to jingle in their pocket. Sometimes they quarreled over their money problems and everyone in the village could hear them shouting. Still, this couple was rather fond of one another, and most of the time they were happy.

One evening Lukrecia came home much earlier than her husband and went to the hearth to light the fire. "It's pointless, really," she said to herself. "It's not as if I have anything to cook. Well, except for a little soup, I suppose. I can't let my dear husband starve."

Lukrecia had just tossed a few logs onto the fire and set the kettle to boil when her husband came home. He settled himself before the blaze and took off his shoes. "Come here, Wife, and sit beside me," said Kazimerz. "It's autumn and the night is cold."

"What news do you bring from the village?" asked Lukrecia.

"Now there's a story," said her husband. "As I was coming home from the market, I saw in the distance a strange object on the road."

"What was it?"

"I couldn't tell, not until I got closer. And when I did, guess what I saw! A fine gold carriage pulled by six large cats."

"You don't say!" exclaimed Lukrecia. "Who would be pulled in such a strange vehicle?"

"*Saule,* she called herself, and a tiny little woman she was," said Kazimerz. "She was dressed like a grand queen."

"Well what was she doing in the middle of the road?"

"You know how the roads get this time of year. I usually don't travel them myself because they get so muddy. She must not have known this, for the tiny woman's carriage was stuck fast in the mud, and even the cats were mired," said the husband.

"So what did you do?"

"The woman didn't want to get out of the carriage herself, dressed as fine as she was, and she asked if I could help. I was afraid to, of course. I thought for sure she was a witch or an evil faerie. When she saw that I was about to run away, she offered a reward for my help."

"A reward!" said Lukrecia, not sure if she believed her husband's tale.

"And I suppose you took her up on it."

"Indeed. I know how poor we are, and I hunger for more than soup for my evening meal. So I grabbed hold of the lead cat, a fearsome creature to behold, and pulled them all out of the mud. The faerie woman, or whatever she was, asked me if I was married and if I were rich. I told her yes to the first and no to the second. 'I can change all that,' she said. 'I will give you three wishes.' Before I could say yea or nay, she was gone."

"What a fool you are, Kazimerz! Wishes my eye! She should have paid you in valuable coin. What nonsense! A faerie! Whoever heard of such a thing!" Lukrecia rose to stir the soup, her back to her husband. "How cruel of you to get my hopes up!"

"We should at least try wishing for something," said her husband miserably. "Then we'll know if the woman spoke true."

Without thinking Lukrecia snapped, "If you're so hungry for more than soup, then I wish we had something else to serve you besides this meager broth. I wish for fat sausages and hearty bread!" No sooner were the words spoken than a feast was spread on the table. There were rich, savory sausages, breads, cheeses and strong beer to be had.

"A finer feast I've never seen!" said Kazimerz in awe. "But, wife, we must be more responsible with the remaining wishes. I don't think we should waste them like this." Then he reached across the table for a slice of bread, knocking the platter of sausages to the floor.

"Kazimerz, you dolt!" shouted Lukrecia. "Look what you've done. I wish that sausage would grow on your face instead of your nose. Then everyone will know you for the idiot I married!" Before she could take back her words, a great sausage was stuck to the middle of her husband's face, right where his nose once sat.

"Lukrecia!" wailed her husband. "Now look what you've done! That's the second wish you wasted. Now we'll have to use the third wish to get rid of this thing."

"But what about fancy clothes? Or fine horses? What about gold and silver dishes, and large houses? There are so many things to wish for. Can't we just cut off the sausage?"

"No, we cannot!" shouted Kazimerz. "I would just as soon cut off my finger or my big toe! You'll have to wish for the sausage to return to the platter. At least we'll get one fine meal from the lady."

"But Kazimerz...."

"Wish it away! I can't go to the village with this thing dangling from my face. And I'm sure you'll never again kiss me with such a nose as this." They shouted at one another for a long while, but in the end Lukrecia knew what she must do.

"Fine. I wish the sausage to return to the platter," she grumbled. And there it was. They both sat at the table and made a hearty meal of the sausage, the cheese, and the bread. They drank many a glass of the strong, rich beer, and when they woke up on the morning they were just as poor as ever.

The King's Son-in-Law

Long ago snakes were held sacred by the Poles and were seen as the spirit of both the hearth and the bathhouse (a sauna-type building where women often gave birth). As such, snakes often appear in folktales of miraculous births.

Long ago in the back of beyond, beyond the seven seas and beyond their farthest shores, there lived a man and a woman. Time passed quickly, as time is wont to do, and the blush of youth in their cheeks gradually faded to grey, and their hair turned white as goose feathers. But in all the years they spent together, they never had any children. They fell to bickering, and the old woman was forever scolding the old man. "Who will look after us when we grow too old to take care of ourselves?" she'd grumble.

"What do you want me to do about it?" the old man would snap back.

"Find us a child! A strong son or a pretty daughter."

To gain himself a little peace, the old man agreed to do just that. So early the next morning he arose, stiff and sore, and took his axe and his journeyman's sack, and headed out into the woods. "Where am I supposed to find a child?" he complained, although there was no one to hear him. "I'll stay out here for three days and three nights. By then my good wife will have forgotten all about this foolish idea, and will welcome me home."

And so he stayed in the woods for three days and three nights, sleeping on the cold, hard ground and eating nothing but bread and butter from his journeyman's sack. "Enough is enough," he grumbled on the dawn of the third morning. "It is time to go home."

On his way home he chanced to see a tiny, jewel-colored snake in the path. "Now that's a marvel!" he thought. "It may not be a child of our own, but perhaps my wife will be delighted with this pretty creature." So he picked up the snake and tucked it into the pocket of his coat. When he finally made it back to the cottage, he found that his wife, rather than being disappointed, was quite charmed by the snake.

"What a darling!" she cooed. "We will feed him fresh milk and soft bread. Get me some at once, Husband." Then she made a bed for the snake out of soft skins and set it by the fire.

Time passed, as time is wont to do, and the snake grew big and strong. Living with humans as he was, he picked up their speech and even thought of the couple as his parents. "Father," he said one day, "I think I would like to marry the king's daughter. Offer him whatever he wants, I will pay the price."

"Then I shall go and ask for her hand," said the old man, unwilling to deny his foster son anything. The next morning he packed his journeyman's sack, tucked the snake into his pocket and headed for the king's palace, which was many leagues hence. Not for a moment did he really expect to be allowed into the court, so it was with much surprise that he found himself in the king's presence.

"My lord," the old man bowed low, "I bring you my blessings."

"I thank you, Old Man," said the king. "Why is it you have journeyed so far from your home to see me?"

"I have come to propose an alliance!" stated the old man.

"An alliance?" laughed the king. "You are a peasant. What benefit can you offer me? You have no army, no land, no wealth. There is nothing I need from you."

"I propose an alliance by marriage, my king. If you give me your daughter for my son, I promise to give you anything you want in return."

"Old Man," the king said sternly, no longer laughing, "I will give you my daughter only on the following condition: That you level the forest which surrounds this castle, plough it for me, and sow it with wheat — all by tomorrow at sunrise. Only then can I accept a peasant for a son-in-law. Do you accept?"

"I accept," sighed the old man, for pride would let him do nothing else.

"You must also bring me a cake of sweet milk made from the grain you harvest," the king continued, "then you shall be allowed to take my daughter."

The old man left the castle, tears streaming down his face. "Why do you weep, Father?" asked the snake poking his head from the old man's coat pocket.

"You heard the king," sobbed the father. "How can I possibly cut down this entire forest, sow wheat and make a cake from the grain by sunrise? It's a fool's errand we've made."

"Oh, don't worry about that," shrugged the snake. "That's a simple matter. You go to sleep and I'll manage the task."

So the old man went to bed and dreamed of fields of ripe grain. And the snake? Why, I suppose he must have gone into the forest, cut down all the trees, sowed grain and watched it grow, for by sunrise, when the old man awoke, a cake of sweet milk was baking over the fire. He immediately dressed and brought the cake to the king.

"Here," he said as he handed over the cake, "I have done all you asked." When the king saw the miracle before him, he was quite impressed, but he loved his daughter dearly and was loathe to see her go.

"I have one more task for you," he said. "Make me a bridge that will span the distance from my castle to your cottage. I want it of solid gold with fruit trees growing all along its length. Then I will be able to visit my daughter any time I wish. Can you have it done by morning?"

The old man sighed and returned to his camp where his foster son was waiting.

"Why are you crying, Father?" asked the snake. "We have accomplished all that the king wished."

"There's more!" said the old man. "Now the king wants a wonder bridge built from the castle to our house so that he may visit his daughter. And he wants it done by morning!"

"I can understand that," said the snake. "For the king loves his daughter almost as much as I do. You go to sleep, and I'll see that the bridge is built." The snake must have kept his word, for as the first rays of dawn lit the land, they glimmered and sparkled off a newly made bridge of gold. Fruit trees of every hew and description lined the route. It was the wonder of the age!

"Good morning, Father-in-Law," said the snake, slithering up to where the king stood by the castle gates.

"Good morning, Son-in-Law," said the king. If he was surprised to find that his daughter was to marry a snake, he did not let it show.

"Where is my new husband, Father?" asked a soft, sweet voice. All eyes turned to see a beautiful maiden approach her father's side. "Who are you talking to?"

"Down here, Beloved," said the snake. "I am to be your bridegroom."

If the princess was surprised at this turn of events, she did not show it, for she was every bit her father's daughter.

"Don't be afraid, Beautiful One," said the jewel-colored snake, pleased that his bride did not run off screaming; or worse, trod him into the ground. "Give me a kiss, my darling, and our engagement will be official."

The princess only hesitated a moment, then leaned down to kiss the little snake. Suddenly the snake flipped in the air, and twisted to-and-fro on the ground. "What have I done?" cried the princess. "Have I somehow hurt him?"

"Hush, Daughter," murmured the king. "There is strange magic afoot."

The snake continued to squirm and twist on the ground, and then he loomed large, aye larger than the old man who bent worriedly over him. When he finally stopped trembling, all the crowd could see that where a snake once stood there was now a handsome knight dressed in shining armor and carrying a powerful sword. He scooped up the maiden in his arms and kissed her soundly. "My brave darling!" he cried. "You kissed me when you could have killed me, and so broke my enchantment. Come now, my love, and we will go to live in my father's cabin in the woods. I cannot wait for Mother to see me — and to meet you!"

The maiden blushed most becomingly, and said to her father, "I think you should call the priest, my lord, there's to be a wedding this day." And so the marriage feast was held, and a great many people were there. The happy couple lived for many years together in the tiny cottage in the woods. They had many children and taught each and every one of them to be kind to all creatures, great and small, for you could never tell who might be trapped in the shape of a beast.

The Three Brothers

There was once upon a time an enchantress who, in the shape of a hawk, would fly to the village of Zakopane and break all the windows of the little church. No sooner would the congregation work to replace the windows than the wretched bird would return. It all seemed rather hopeless.

In this same village there lived three brothers, Alaryk, Bronislaw and Kaspek, who were all determined to kill the mischievous hawk. But it was in vain that the two eldest would keep watch outside the church with their guns. As soon as the bird appeared high above their heads a magical sleep overpowered them. They would not awake until they heard the beautiful stained glass come crashing to the ground below.

Then the youngest brother, Kaspek, took his turn at guarding the windows. To prevent being overcome by sleep he placed a necklace of thorns around his neck. When teased by his brothers he replied, "If I feel the least bit drowsy and begin to nod my head, why, these thorns will quickly prick my neck and wake me in an instant!"

The moon was already risen, and it was as light as day when Kaspek heard a fierce screeching from above. At the same time a terrible desire to sleep swept over him. His eyelids closed, and his head sank on his shoulders, but the thorns sank deep and were so painful that he awoke at once. He saw the hawk swooping down from the sky. Quicker than thought, he took aim with his gun and fired. The hawk, shot through the wing, fell like a stone behind the church.

Kaspek ran to the back to recover it, but it was nowhere to be found. Instead, a huge hole had opened in the ground. It was deep, aye, deeper than the mining pits near the village. He went at once to fetch his brothers and with their help dragged a lot of pinewood and ropes to the spot.

"We must explore the abyss and find the enchantress," he told them. "Only then can we be sure that the windows are safe."

They fastened some of the burning pine to the end of the rope, and let it slowly down to the bottom of the pit. At first it was quite dark and the flaming torch only lit up dirty grey stone walls. But Kaspek was determined to explore the abyss. "Let me down on another rope," he said. "I will follow the torch."

Down, down, down he went, deep into the earth. Below him a light began to form which quickly grew as bright as the sun. When he reached the bottom of the pit, he found a lovely meadow full of green trees and fragrant flowers.

In the middle of the meadow stood a huge stone castle with an iron gate leading to it. The gate was wide open in welcome. Kaspek went up to the entrance, more awed than afraid, and opened the great bronze doors. Everything in the castle seemed to be made of copper, from the stairs which led away to unknown corridors to the wall sconces which cast their bright, coppery flames.

"How strange," murmured Kaspek. "In such a marvelous castle I find no one to welcome me."

He began to search the rooms of the castle, one by one. High in a tower overlooking the meadows, he discovered a girl combing her long titian tresses. Kaspek noticed that whenever one of her hairs fell on the ground it rang out like pure metal. He peered at the maiden more closely and saw that her skin was smooth and fair, her tawny eyes bright and sparkling, and her hair as brilliant as the sun. He fell in love with her on the spot.

"Hello," he whispered, falling to one knee. "I have come to ask you to be my wife."

"I am Florentyna. I would follow you, and gladly," said the maiden, "but I am kept a prisoner in this land. I cannot travel to the world above until my mother, the enchantress, is dead. She has jealously guarded my sisters and me for all of these years. She kills anyone who attempts to take us away. I will understand if you find it necessary to return alone. She is terrible to behold."

"I am not afraid of her," said Kaspek. "I have already wounded your mother."

"Wounded, but not killed. The only way to do that is if you use the sword which hangs on the wall of the great room. Only, the sword is so heavy that I've never known anyone who could lift it," she added.

Vowing to return soon, Kaspek made his way down the hall until he reached a chamber where everything inside was made of silver. Here he found another beautiful girl, the sister of his bride. She was combing her moonlit tresses, and every hair that fell on the ground rang out like pure metal.

"Your sister has sent me," he said by way of introduction. "I have come for the silver sword."

The second girl pointed to the sword on the wall, but though he tried with all his strength he could not lift it.

"It is hopeless," he gasped. "We will have to find something else to defeat your mother."

A third sister entered the room carrying a bottle of elixir. "Here," she said, "this is the Water of Life. Drink it down, it will give you the strength you need."

Kaspek drank one drop, but still he could not lift the sword. Then he drank a second drop, and the sword began to move. Only after he had drunk a third drop was he able to swing the sword over his head.

"Hurry," urged the sisters, "our mother will be here soon."

Kaspek hid himself in the castle and awaited the arrival of the old crone. At last, as it was beginning to grow dark, she appeared. She swooped down upon a big apple tree and, after shaking some of the golden apples from it, she pounced down upon the earth. Her wing appeared to be healed and Kaspek knew that nothing but the sword would kill this witch.

As soon as her feet touched the ground, she was transformed from a hawk into a woman. This was the moment the youth was waiting for, and he swung his mighty sword in the air with all his strength and whack! chopped the witch's head clean off her shoulders.

"Now we can travel to the surface," said his beloved.

Kaspek asked the maidens to help him pack up the treasures of the castle. When everything of value was tucked into three great trunks, he pulled on the rope to give his brothers a signal to pull them up out of the abyss. First the treasures were atttached to the rope and then the three lovely girls. Soon, everything had been been taken to the surface, and only he himself remained below.

A nagging worm of suspicion ate at his heart. Sick with dread and suddenly fearful of trusting his brothers, Kaspek tied a heavy stone onto the rope and let them pull it up. At first they heaved with a will, but when the stone was halfway up Bronislaw and Alaryk let it drop. It fell to the bottom, broken in a hundred pieces.

"So that's what would have happened to my bones had I trusted myself to them," said the youth sadly, and he began to cry bitterly. He cared not a whit for the fine treasures, but he feared he would never again see his lovely girl with her swan-like neck and golden hair.

For a long while he wandered sadly all through the beautiful underworld. One day he met a magician who asked him the cause of his tears. Kaspek told him all that had befallen him, and the magician said, "Do not grieve, young man! If you will guard my children who are hidden in the golden apple tree, I will bring you at once up to the earth. There is another magician who always eats my children up whenever he can find them. It is in vain that I have hidden the last two under the earth and locked them into the castle. Now I have hidden them in the apple tree. Hide yourself there, too, and at midnight you will see my enemy."

"Why do you not use your powers to stop him?" asked Kaspek.

"Unfortunately his magic is stronger than mine," said the father, "only bravery and strength will save my children."

The youth climbed up the tree and picked some of the beautiful golden apples, which he shared with the magician's children. And then they waited.

At midnight the wind began to rise, and a rustling sound was heard at the foot of the tree. Kaspek looked down and beheld a long thick serpent beginning to crawl up the tree. It wound itself around the stem and gradually got higher and higher. It stretched its huge head among the branches, searching with its glittering eyes for the nest in which the little children lay. They trembled with terror when they saw the hideous creature, and hid themselves beneath the leaves.

Then Kaspek swung his silver sword in the air, and with one blow cut off the serpent's head. He cut up the rest of the body into little bits and strewed them to the four winds.

The father of the rescued children was so delighted over the death of his enemy that he said to Kaspek, "I will transform myself into an eagle. Climb on my back and I will take you to the upper world."

With what joy did Kaspek hurry now to his brothers' house! He burst into the room where they were all assembled, but no one knew who he was. Only his bride, who was serving as cook to her sisters, recognized her lover at once.

Alaryk and Bronislaw, who had quite believed he was dead, yielded up his treasures to him at once, and flew into the woods in terror. But the good youth forgave them all they had done, and divided his treasures with them. Then he built himself a big castle with golden windows, and there he lived happily with his Florentyna, his golden-haired wife, till the end of their days.

The Crow

Once upon a time there were three maidens, sisters they were, and each of them young and beautiful. Teodora, although she was not fairer than the other two, was the most loveable and charming of them all.

About half-a-mile from their home stood a castle, ancient and crumbling. It was so long uninhabited that no one could even remember the name of the family which once lived there. Yet the gardens still possessed some of their former beauty, and wild roses grew in abundance amongst the rocks and ruin. In this garden Teodora would stroll along the paths and dream the dreams of youth.

One day when she was pacing to-and-fro under the linden trees, a black crow hopped out of a rosebush in front of her. The poor beast was all torn and bleeding. "You poor thing!" crooned Teodora. "What has happened to you?"

The bird cocked his head and gazed up at the maiden with his tiny, black eyes. "I am not really a crow," he said, "but an enchanted prince who has been doomed to spend his youth in misery."

"What can I do to help?" asked the kindhearted girl.

"If only you knew what you offered!" sighed the bird. "No, it is too much to ask of anyone."

"No, I insist," said Teodora.

"If you wished, my dear, you could save me. But you would have to say good-bye to all your own people and come and be my constant companion in this ruined castle. That is part of the curse; I can only be saved by a willing maiden."

"Well, that you have found," smiled Teodora kindly.

"There is one habitable room in the castle," the crow continued, "in it is a golden bed. There you will have to live all by yourself. And don't forget that whatever you may see or hear in the night you must not scream out, for if you give as much as a single cry my suffering is doubled."

The sweet-natured maiden returned home only long enough to bid good-bye to her sisters and to pack what few belongings she possessed.

Then she hurried to the ruined castle and took possession of the room with the golden bed.

When night approached she lay down, but though she shut her eyes tight sleep would not come. At midnight she heard to her great horror someone coming along the passage. In a minute her door was flung wide open and a troop of strange beings entered the room. A fire roared to life in the huge fireplace, and a great cauldron was set to boil. When they had done this, the creatures approached the bed on which the trembling girl lay and, screaming and yelling all the time, dragged her toward the cauldron.

"What a fine maiden we'll dine on tonight!" they cackled to one another.

"It's been many a day since we shared such a tasty morsel," said another.

Teodora nearly died with fright, but she remembered the crow's words and never uttered a sound. It was as she felt the heat of the boiling water touch her face that the cock called out the dawn and all the spirits vanished.

At that same moment, the crow appeared and hopped all round the room with joy. "Thank you! Thank you!" he crowed. "Because of your kindness, my suffering has already been lessened."

So Teodora spent her days in solitude. At night she would have been frightened had she not been so brave. She never once cried out in fear and every morning the crow came and thanked her for her endurance, and assured her that his sufferings were far less than they had been.

And so two years passed away. One day the crow came to the maiden and said, "In another year I shall be freed from the spell I am under, because then the seven-year curse will be over. But before I can resume my natural form and take possession of the belongings of my forefathers, you must go out into the world and take service as a maidservant. This too is part of the curse."

Teodora consented at once, and for a whole year she served as a maid. In spite of her youth and beauty, she was very badly treated, and suffered a great many things. One evening, when she was spinning flax and had worked her little white hands weary, she heard a rustling beside her and a cry of joy. Then she saw a handsome youth standing beside her, who knelt down at her feet and kissed the little weary hands.

"I am the prince," he said, "the one you in your goodness, when I was wandering about in the shape of a black crow, freed from the most awful torments. Come now to my castle with me, and let us live there happily together."

So they went to the castle where they had both endured so much. But when they reached it, it was difficult to believe that it was the same, for it had all been rebuilt and was like new. And there they lived for a hundred years, always as happy as the day when the curse was lifted.

Iskrzycki the Firestone

There came to the King of Krakow a stranger who called himself Iskrzycki the Firestone. "I wish to be in your employ," he said.

"I can always use a good pair of hands," said the king. "Let us draw up a contract of service." A contract was drawn up, witnessed and signed. It was only then that the king noticed that instead of feet Iskrzycki had two horses' hooves.

"I demand that we break this agreement at once!" said the king. "I have been deceived. You're not even human!"

"You never asked," said Iskrzycki. "I stand by my rights. The contract will not be broken." And because there were many witnesses, the king was forced to agree.

From that moment on Iskrzycki took up residence in the castle stove. There he kept it rather hot, so that the cook never needed to build a fire. All the kitchen staff grew accustomed to his presence, as did most of the castle. Everyone, that is, except for the queen.

"He's a most unnatural creature," she would complain to her husband.

"I am uncomfortable whenever he passes by. I can feel the heat from him, and always fear that my clothes will catch afire!"

"Then we'll retire to our summer residence," said the king, ever conscious of his wife's happiness. The entire court packed up to leave, and a great procession of carriages and horses left Krakow. They had traveled most of the day and into the early evening when the peacefulness of dusk was shattered by the queen's high-pitched screams. All eyes turned to see the royal carriage tottering on the edge of a cliff, having given way to the road's edge.

"Have no fear, my lady! Iskrzycki is with you!" called a voice from behind the carriage. And before anyone else could make a move to rescue the royal couple, Iskrzycki had pushed the carriage safely back onto the road.

The king and queen knew that they would not be able to leave the Firestone behind. So they turned the procession around and returned to the city, where Iskrzycki served them for many long and faithful years.

Midsummer's Eve

At the summer solstice, the waxing sun reaches its highest point before beginning its slide into darkness. It is the longest day of the year, and at one time was the most important and widespread of the pre-Christian festivals celebrated from Ireland to Russia. In folklore traditions, the night before the solstice, Midsummer's Eve, is a time of great magic — especially for love spells and divinations. Sorceresses and fairies roam about on Midsummer's Eve and great bonfires are lit to lend strength to the sun. In the Slavic countries, young men would leap over the bonfire to show their courage, and maidens would make garlands of nine sacred herbs. These would be cast into the river to ask the blessings of Kupaya, the Water Mother. If a youth was fortunate enough to catch hold of one of these floral wreaths, he could claim the maiden as his own.

Tomislaw watched the other men with envy. How he wished that he had two strong legs to leap across the fire! That would surely impress Jolanta, whom he had loved since childhood. But it was not to be. A threshing accident had left him with a bad limp. So he sat, angry and helpless outside the circle of firelight beneath the spreading branches of a linden tree.

"Why are you so sad, Little One?" asked a voice from above. Tomislaw looked up to see a woman sitting in the branches above his head. Bright blue eyes shone with merriment in a face lined by age. Long black hair, streaked with silver, flowed about her shoulders.

"Who are you?" asked Tomislaw.

"Do you really need to ask? Tsk! Tsk! I'm a *Kupaya*, it is I whom you honor this evening."

"You are mistaken," said Tomislaw bitterly. "As you can see I am not a whole man. I will not be leaping across the fire or swimming in the river to catch Jolanta's garland."

"For shame, Child!" laughed *Kupaya*. "Did you think I would forget any of my children this evening?"

"What do you want from me?"

"Go into the forest, Tomislaw, now, while everyone else is busy with the festivities. There gather the fire flower of the fern. It has the power to grant wishes."

"Ha!" sneered Tomislaw, "you wish to make a fool of me, too. Everyone knows that ferns do not flower."

"On this night they do," said *Kupaya*. "At the precise stroke of midnight. Now go, and do not listen to the voices that would seek to lead you astray."

Tomislaw limped down the path into the forest knowing just where a fern plant was to be found. It was not long before he came upon it, and he sat down to wait for the hour of midnight. All around him the trees moved about in the shadows, pulling themselves up from their roots to get a closer view.

"What are you doing, Tomislaw?" one asked in a voice like dry twigs crackling on the fire.

"It is hopeless, Tomislaw. You will never get the flower," said another.

"Go back, Tomislaw, go back before it is too late," said a third. "The flower will never bring you happiness."

"She will never love you, Tomislaw," said a fourth tree. And it was those words that hurt most of all.

At the first stroke of midnight, a bud appeared on the fern. With each passing stroke it grew bigger, until finally at the exact hour of midnight, it burst open with a light so brilliant that the clearing was suddenly as bright as day. Tomislaw, swallowing his fear and ignoring the jeers of the trees around him, plucked the blossom from the fern. A voice boomed across the clearing, "What is it you wish, Tomislaw?"

The lad thought about Jolanta, the beautiful maiden who had never once returned his love. He thought about his parents and knew they considered him a burden. He thought about all the other men in the village who mocked him for his weakness. Tomislaw thought about a great many things in that brief moment. And then he said, without hesitation, "I wish to be very rich. I want to live far away in one of the great cities, where I never need to think about this cursed village again."

"It is so," the voice thundered.

Tomislaw got his wish. He lived in a great city in a large house with many servants. He threw lavish parties and mingled with all of the other wealthy people. He should have been very happy, but he was not. He felt more miserable and alone than ever.

He began to dream of his old village. He missed his family. He missed the fragrant fields and forests. And though he scorned himself for his weakness, he missed Jolanta. He decided to visit the home of his youth.

He had not been back in the village since that long ago Midsummer's Eve, and he found that much had changed. When he came to his father's old cottage, no one recognized him in his fine clothes and fancy carriage.

"Good day to you, Sir," a young man bowed, and Tomislaw recognized his youngest brother who had been but a child when he left.

"Do you not recognize me, Jacek?" he said. "It is I, Tomislaw. I've come home. Where are Mother and Father?"

"Tomislaw? We all thought you were dead. Where have you been all of these years? Mother and Father died a long time ago. The crops had failed, and a famine swept through our village. Our parents starved to death that winter. Until the very end they wondered what happened to you, and missed you very much. Where were you?"

"Dead? They're dead? And what of Jolanta?" asked Tomislaw. "Whatever happened to her?"

"She was waiting for you on the night you disappeared. She was waiting for you to catch her garland in the river. She always loved you, you know."

"What happened to her?" Tomislaw repeated.

"She died of heartache when she heard you vanished. She would not accept the love of any other, and she died of a lonely heart."

"Aye, me!" cried Tomislaw. "What a fool I've been! I should have shared the bounty of *Kupaya's* gift, rather than keep it to myself. So much sadness! So much loss!"

Sadly, the rich man returned to his fine home in the city where he soon died of regret, realizing that no one can be truly happy without sharing that happiness with others.

The Dragon

In most Eastern European myths the Baba Yaga *(known in Poland as the* Jezi Baba) *is a man-eating crone who lives in a hut on the edge of the forest. The cottage stands on chicken legs which lower and rise at the* Jezi Baba's *command. The crone travels around in a giant mortar, using a pestle in her right hand to steer her course and a broom in her left hand to wipe away the tracks. In early folklore, the* Jezi Baba *was a good faerie, only later was she described as an ugly old witch, and her stories used to frighten young children.*

There was once a great war that tore across the countryside. Many villages were destroyed, and many people were killed. It was also an expensive war. The king had a great many soldiers, but he was unable to pay them very much. He was not able to feed them at all. In those days it was not profitable to be a soldier.

There were three soldiers who decided to desert. "If we are caught, they will hang us," said Wilhelm, the oldest of the trio. "How shall we get away without anyone taking notice?"

"We will hide in the cornfield," said Benek, the second eldest. "No one will find us in there."

"A fine plan," said Andrzejek, the youngest of the men. "Tomorrow the army marches on. By the time we are missed, it will be too late. They will not send anyone after us."

They hid themselves in the field and waited until dawn. But the army did not march on as expected. They remained as they were, scattered all around the field. For two days and two nights the deserters hid in the corn and grew so hungry that they nearly died.

"If only this corn were ripe!" said Benek. "We would not be so hungry then."

"Perhaps we should just return to camp," said Wilhelm. "We may be able to scrounge up some food there."

"Don't be a fool," said Andrzejek. "If we venture out it will be certain death."

They hid in the corn for another day and another night. "What was the use of our deserting?" grumbled Benek. "We will die here for sure."

Before the others could say anything, a fiery dragon swooped down from the night sky. It hovered above them and asked, "Why do you cower in this field? What is it that you fear?"

Andrzejek answered, "We are three soldiers who deserted our posts because our pay was so small. Now if we remain here we will die of hunger, and if we return to camp we will be strung up on the gallows."

"Hmmm," mused the dragon, stroking his beard, "if you will serve me for seven years, I will lead you through the middle of the army so that no one will catch you."

"Will you feed us?" asked Andrzejek.

"What kind of master would I be if I did not? You will have bread and ale aplenty."

"We have no choice, Men," said Andrzejek. "We must accept this dragon's offer."

The dragon scooped the three men up with his claws, flew with them high over the heads of the surrounding army and gently set them down on the earth. He gave them each a little sack. "In it you will find coins enough to spare and more. Go, live as kings for now, but after seven years you are mine. Sign my contract now and we will part ways."

Then he put a parchment in front of them. Benek and Wilhelm signed it immediately, but Andrzejek paused to consider. "I fear you have tricked us, Dragon. For you said we were to be your servants for seven years. You did not say we would be rich for seven years and then come back to you."

"You misunderstood," said the dragon smoothly. "But I will make another deal with you. Sign now, and listen carefully. At the end of seven years I will give you a riddle. If you can guess it you shall be free, and I will trouble you no more."

"Agreed then," said Andrzejek, and he too signed the parchment. The dragon flew away, and the three men left, carrying their sacks of gold. They now had as much money as they wanted, wore fine clothes, and lived in large castles. The seven years passed quickly away, and when the time was nearly ended, two of them grew ever more frightened.

"What have we done!" cried Benek. "If we had stayed in the army, the war would be over, and we would be back on our homesteads married to a pretty farm girl."

"We never should have left!" wailed Wilhelm. "We are to spend the remainder of our days in service to a demon dragon. What is to become of us?"

"Don't trouble yourselves," laughed Andrzejek. "I consider myself a clever man. I will answer the riddle."

The three of them returned to the spot where they had last seen the dragon. An old woman passed by and asked them why they were so sad.

"Go away, Old Woman!" said Benek. "What business is it of yours? You cannot possibly help us."

"Who knows?" she cackled. "Tell me your troubles and we shall see."

Andrzejek knew it was the *Jezi Baba*, the crone enchantress, who spoke to them now. Without fear he told her that they had become the servants of the dragon. "For seven long years we have lived like kings, and money has been as plentiful as stars in the sky. But now we wait for the dragon to return."

"And I suppose the dragon has given you a riddle," said the *Jezi Baba*. "If you are as clever as you look, you would have sought a way to break the agreement."

"He has," laughed Andrzejek. "Can you help?"

"I am willing to help you because you are brave and smart. If it were not for you, I would leave your friends to their miserable fate. Yes, I have a plan."

She told the men that one of them should journey into the woods. "There you will find a tumbledown heap of rocks which looks like a little house. Go inside, and find what help is offered."

"What good would that do, Old Woman?" sneered Wilhelm. "I'm not going anywhere."

"And I will certainly not set foot into the woods alone," added Benek. "There might be bears or wolves or robbers waiting for me!"

But Andrzejek jumped up and headed straight into the woods. There he found the stone hut, just where the *Jezi Baba* said it would be. In the hut stood a very old woman, older even than the *Jezi Baba*.

"Good morning, Grandmother," said Andrzejek.

"Who are you?" she demanded angrily. "What is your business with me?"

Andrzejek poured out the entire story to the old woman. "Ah," she nodded when the tale was done, "that is my grandson you speak of, the dragon. A little mischief-maker is that one. He should be taught not to meddle in the affairs of others. Yes, I will help you."

With that she lifted a large grey stone which covered the entrance to her cellar. "Hide yourself in there young man, you should be able to hear everything from there. But don't make a sound and don't move a muscle! My grandson is to visit me shortly."

Within the hour, the dragon flew in. "Grandmother!" he called, "might I beg a bit of supper? I am on my way to pick up my new servants."

The old woman set the table and brought out meat and wine. "So tell me about these new servants," she said. "I don't think you've mentioned them before."

"Three soldiers, they are! What fine servants they will make. I have given them the opportunity to escape, of course, but they will never be able to answer my riddle."

"A riddle?" asked the old woman innocently. "Why don't you tell me. You know how I do so love a good riddle."

"All right, Grandmother. In the Baltic Sea lies a dead sea-cat — that shall be their roast meat, and beside it lies the rib of a whale — that shall be their silver spoon; next to that is the hollow foot of a dead horse — that shall be their wineglass."

When the dragon had gone to take a nap, his old grandmother pulled up the stone and let out the soldier. "Did you hear everything?" she asked. "Yes, every word," said Andrzejek. Then he crawled past the sleeping dragon and out the door. In haste he made his way back to his companions. He told them how the dragon had been outfoxed by his grandmother, and how he had heard from the dragon's own lips the answer to the riddle. Then they were all delighted and in high spirits.

"There is hope for us yet!" cried Benek and Wilhelm.

Just then the dragon swooped down from the sky holding the parchment in his clawed fist. Without even a "good evening, gentlemen," he pointed out their signatures and said, "Follow me underground, to my home. There I shall feed you. If you can tell me what you will get for your roast meat, you shall be free — and I will let you keep the bottomless sacks of gold."

When they went down to the dragon's lair, Benek said, "In the Baltic Sea lies a dead sea-cat. That is what we shall have for our roast meat."

The dragon was, of course, greatly irritated, but he covered it well and said to Wilhelm, "Ah, but what shall you have as your spoon?" Two servants were, after all, better than none.

"The rib of a whale shall be our silver spoon," Wilhelm promptly replied.

The dragon growled low in his throat before turning to Andrzejek. "Do you know what your wineglass shall be?"

Andrzejek grinned wide. "An old horse's hoof shall be our wineglass," he said.

"Who helped you?" shrieked the dragon. "You would never have answered those questions on your own!"

"The *Jezi Baba* helped us," said Andrzejek. "And your own grandmother betrayed you."

With another shriek the dragon flew into the night sky. He no longer had any power over the soldiers, and the contract was broken. Benek, Wilhelm and Andrzejek returned to the city with their sacks of gold, and lived happily there the rest of their lives.

The Cow of Krakow

In the days now long departed, so far back that no one can say quite when, there lived in the city of Krakow a poor family named Jaskula. They had a roof over their head, but little else, only a cow named Olenka who provided them with all of the milk and cream they could want. One day the landlord came by demanding that they pay the rent.

"We cannot," said the father. "Business has been poor, and we do not even have enough money to buy bread. It is only because of our dear cow Olenka that we have survived at all."

"Then you must sell me the cow," said the landlord.

"I cannot, my youngest daughter is sick. She needs the milk our cow provides."

"Sell me your cow," the landlord repeated, "or else you and all your children will find themselves sleeping in the streets this evening."

It was winter and cold as only winters in Poland can be. It would break the father's heart to have his children sleeping outside. His daughter would die for sure. Sighing heavily, he agreed to sell Olenka.

The landlord took the cow to his own shed, dreaming of the rich cream and butter he would have each meal. But Olenka became sick, and her milk dried up. The landlord decided to consult the local *babci*, the wise old crone who lived near the market. "I think she is sick," he told the *babci*. "What is the matter? Can she be cured?"

"The cow is enchanted," said the *babci*. "She will give milk only to those who are in need."

"But I am in need!" insisted the landlord. "I need fresh milk each morning or else I will have to walk to the market to buy it."

"That is not true need, as you well know. Where is your spirit of *tloka*, of neighborly compassion? Go, return the cow to its rightful home. Go, or else the cow and your poor neighbors will probably all die."

The landlord refused to give the cow back. Shortly after that, he was struck by a passing wagon and died on the spot. Everyone in the neighborhood agreed; it was the will of the *zorya*, the sister of fate.

As for Olenka? The cow eventually wandered back to the Jaskula home where she gave milk as freely as before.

The Giants

Little Romek had neither father nor mother. Like many orphans in those long gone days he had two choices: to work or to starve. Being a very clever boy, he chose to look after the sheep of a rich farmer. Three meals a day and a warm blanket at night! He was very happy, indeed.

Day and night, all through the summer, Romek spent his time in the high pastures. Only when it was very wet and stormy did he take refuge in the shieling on the edge of a big forest. It was a good life, and he did not wish to trade it for anything.

Now one night, when he was sitting beneath the stars with his flock, he heard the sound of someone crying. "Who would be up here?" he wondered. Still wrapped in his blanket he followed the direction of the sobs. To his utter astonishment, he found a giant lying at the edge of the clearing.

"Don't be afraid!" the giant called before Romek could run off. "I won't hurt you!"

"My *babci* always taught me that giants cannot be trusted," said Romek with more bravery than he felt.

"Your *babci* was wrong. It is actually my intent to reward you handsomely if you will bind up my foot. I hurt it when I tripped over one of your sheep."

Romek tore his blanket into strips and bound up the giant's wounds. "Ah, much better," sighed the giant, gingerly putting his full weight on the foot. "Now follow me and I will give you your reward."

"Where are we going?" asked Romek. "I can't leave my sheep behind."

"Don't worry about them," said the giant. "They will come to no harm."

"But where are we going?" asked Romek, still not quite willing to trust a giant.

"To celebrate a wedding. Didn't I say that? There's a marriage today and I promise you it will be fun. But I almost forgot! Wear this band around your waist. It will render you invisible, and my brothers won't be tempted to toss you into the stew pot!"

With these words, he handed Romek a sash with red, black and white embroidery. Instantly Romek vanished except for his shadow. "Don't worry about that," laughed the giant. "No one will notice if there is one shadow too many! Just hold onto my coattail!"

Soon they came to a great hall where a hundred or more giants were assembled. Romek gazed about him in astonishment. "Never would I have believed it possible!" he murmured. "Even the very walls are made of gold!"

All the giants and Romek, too, gathered around the tables or sat in the heavy wooden chairs. There they began to eat and drink. When Romek had eaten and drunk as much as he could, he thought to himself, "Why shouldn't I put a loaf of bread in my pocket? I shall be glad of it tomorrow when I am back with the flock." So he grabbed a loaf when no one was looking and stowed it away under his tunic.

No sooner had he done so than the wounded giant limped up to him and whispered softly, "Shepherd Boy, are you there?"

"Here I am," said Romek. "Right behind you."

"Grab onto my coattail again, and I'll lead you out of here."

Romek returned to his sheep and took off the invisible belt. The giant forgot to ask for it back, and so he hid it carefully in his knapsack. He slept soundly that night, and in the morning thought to cut off a piece of the loaf he had carried away from the wedding feast. Although he tried with all his might, he couldn't tear off even the smallest piece. Then he tried to bite into the bread. Imagine his astonishment when a piece of gold fell out of his mouth and rolled at his feet! He bit the loaf a second time, and then a third, and each time a piece of gold fell out of his mouth. Yet the bread itself remained untouched. Romek was delighted, and hid the magic loaf in his bag.

Now the merchant, whose sheep Romek looked after, had a very lovely daughter, Jozefina, who always smiled and waved to the youth when she walked with her father in his fields. For a long time Romek had been planning a surprise for Jozefina's birthday — only he didn't know what that surprise would be. On the day of her birthday, he put on his invisible belt, took a sack of gold pieces with him, and slipping into her room in the middle of the night, placed the bag of gold beside her bed.

Jozefina was thrilled, as was her thrifty father, when she found the sack of gold. Romek was so delighted to think what happiness he had given the maiden that the next night he placed another bag of gold beside her bed. And this he continued to do for seven nights. "It must be a good fairy who brought the gold," said Jozefina.

"A fairy!" laughed her father. "I don't care who it is, but perhaps we should wait up and see."

On the eighth night a fearful storm of wind and rain arose while the shepherd lad was on his way to the merchant's house. It wasn't until he reached the house that he realized he left his belt of invisibility behind. He didn't like the idea of going back to his hut in the wind and wet, so he just stepped as he was into the girl's room and laid the sack of gold beside her. He was just turning to leave when the merchant confronted him and said, "You young rogue! You were going to steal the gold that a good fairy brings every night, were you?" Romek was so taken aback that he stood trembling before his master and did not even try to explain his presence.

"As you have always behaved well in my service, I will not send you to prison," the merchant continued. "I do not want to be accused of abusing an orphan! But you must leave instantly and never let me gaze on your face again."

Romek went back to his hut, packed his loaf and belt, and traveled to the nearest town. There he bought himself some fine clothes, a beautiful coach with four horses, hired two servants, and drove back to his master. You may imagine how astonished the merchant was to see his shepherd boy return in this manner!

Romek told of the piece of good luck that had befallen him, and asked him for the hand of his beautiful daughter. Before her father could answer, Jozefina said, "Romek, I would have married you anyway, with or without your fortune, only my father chased you out before I could speak." Romek and Jozefina were soon wed and lived together happily all the days of their lives.

The Flower Queen's Daughter

The classical myth of Persephone's abduction by Pluto had spread far and wide, even to the Slavic lands. This is not surprising since worship of the maiden goddess lasted in some parts of Greece well into the nineteenth century. The Greek version told of her abduction into the underworld, when her mother Demeter — later identified as Mother Nature — in her sorrow cast the land into winter. In the springtime Peresphone was allowed to return to her mother, and the world once again became green and growing. In the Slavic version of this story, the Flower Queen is none other than Demeter, while the god of the underworld, Pluto, has been transformed into a fierce dragon.

One day a young prince was riding through a meadow that stretched for miles in front of him when he came to a deep open ditch. He was turning aside to avoid it when he heard the sound of someone crying. Dismounting from the back of his destrier, he cautiously moved in the direction from which the sound came. To his astonishment he found an old woman who begged him to help her out of the ditch. The prince bent down and lifted her out of her living grave, asking "However did you manage this, Old Woman?"

"Oh, my son," she said. "I am but a poor old woman. Soon after midnight, I had set out for the neighboring town in order to sell my eggs in the market. But I lost my way in the dark and fell into this deep ditch. I would have remained here forever if it were not for the kindness of the *Zorya*. It was they that have sent you to me."

"You can hardly walk in your condition," the prince shook his head. "Hop on my horse, I will carry you home. Is it very far?"

"I live at the edge of the forest with my cat as companion. No more than a morning's distance by foot."

The prince lifted her onto his horse. Soon they reached the hut, a strange looking hut which stood on two chicken legs. It was then that the prince knew he spoke with the *Jezi Baba*.

The *Jezi Baba* jumped down and said to the prince. "Just a minute,

my boy. Don't go anywhere. I have a gift for you." She disappeared into her hut but soon returned. "You're not married yet, are you, Son?"

"No," replied the prince hesitantly.

"And I suppose what you would like is a wife of your own."

"True," he answered.

"One of such beauty and grace as would befit your position," the *Jezi Baba* continued.

"I suppose," he answered.

"Then I know the perfect girl!" the old woman clapped her hands. "The most beautiful girl in the world is the daughter of the Flower Queen."

"Where can I find this maiden?" asked the prince.

"Well," the *Jezi Baba* hesitated, "right now she's somewhat unavailable."

"You mean she's married?"

"No…I mean she's currently living in the cave of a dragon. Not willingly, of course!" she cackled. "But she is in need of rescuing. If you set her free, I'm sure she'd marry you."

"What do you suggest I do?" asked the prince.

"I will give you a little bell. Ring it once, and the King of Ravens will appear. He will be able to help you."

Before the prince could thank the *Jezi Baba*, she had returned to her cottage. Up it rose on its chicken legs and quickly disappeared into the forest.

"The Flower Queen's daughter?" the prince mused. "She is perhaps worth at least a look."

For a whole year he traveled beyond the seven seas and beyond their farthest shores. And while he was hungry and tired and very often cold, he continued his search. At last he came to a tiny cottage at the edge of the world where an old man sat rocking in his chair.

"Can you tell of the dragon who keeps for himself the Flower Queen's daughter?"

"It's the Flower Queen's daughter you're after, is it?" smiled the old man. "Well, I can't tell you where she is, but I can point you to my father's cottage. Perhaps he can help you."

As tired as the prince was, he followed the path deeper into the woods until he reached a second stone cottage. There he found a very old man rocking in his chair. "Have you seen the Flower Queen's daughter or know where she might be found?" asked the prince.

The very old man's face split into a toothless grin. "It's the Flower Queen's daughter you want, is it?" he laughed. "She's a beauty, to be sure."

"Then you've seen her?" the prince asked hopefully.

"No, I haven't," said the very old man. "It was my father that told me of her beauty. If you continue up this road, you will come across his cottage. Ask him yourself."

And so the prince traveled deeper into the woods, and he soon came across the cottage where a very, very old man sat rocking in his chair.

"Have you seen the Flower Queen's daughter or the dragon that keeps her prisoner?"

"I have," said the very, very old man. "So it's the Flower Queen's daughter you seek? She's a beauty. Well, my lad, continue up this path. When you reach the top of the mountain you'll find the dragon's cave."

"Oh, thank you!" cried the prince.

"It's lucky you are, too," continued the old man. "The dragon has just entered his sleep cycle. For six months he sleeps, and for six months he stays awake."

So the prince went up the mountain until he reached a golden castle. There were no guards at the gate so he walked right in. Suddenly an ancient dragon, with flaking scales and dull-edged teeth, swooped down from the heavens. "What do you want in this place?" it growled.

"Who are you?" the prince demanded insolently.

"The dragon's mother," said the winged serpent. "What is your business here?"

"I have heard so much about the grace and beauty and kindness of the dragon's mother," said the prince. "It's pleased I am to finally meet you. I would like to enter your service."

"Flattery will gain you entrance," the dragon's mother preened. "Follow me."

They entered the castle and the dragon's mother sat down. The prince scanned the crowd of attendants, but no one matched the description of the Flower Queen's daughter.

"If you wish to be in my service," said the dragon's mother, "then you must watch after my youngset son. But I warn you, if he does not arrive safely each morning, I will gobble you up for my breakfast and pick my teeth clean with your bones."

Each evening the prince rode out on the dragon youth's back and showed him the ways of the world. Each dawn found them safe and sound in the walls of the castle. On the morning of the third day, the young dragon said, "I grow weary, my friend. Let me land but a moment and stretch." No sooner had the prince climbed down from the dragon's back than the dragon flew up into the sky.

"No!" cried the prince, fearing the dragon mother's wrath. "Come back!" The young dragon was but a speck in the sky, and then he was gone. In desperation the prince remembered the words of the *Jezi Baba*.

"I call to the King of the Ravens!" he shouted. "Come to my aid, I beg!" And then he rang the little bell.

The sound of flapping wings filled the air and a hundred ravens flew through the sky, blocking the sun's rays. In the middle of the group flew the King of Ravens. He landed at the prince's feet and said, "As one noble to another, I greet you."

"I need your help," said the prince. "You see...."

"I already know your plight," said the King of Ravens. "Word of your journey has reached me in my castle in the clouds. You seek the dragon mother's youngest son. Already my attendants have set off after him, and should return shortly."

Quicker said than done, a flock of ravens landed, dragging with them the rebellious dragon youth. "Thank you!" cried the prince. Leaping upon the dragon's back he rode back to the castle.

"You have guarded my son well," said the dragon's mother. "For that you shall be allowed to come to the dance this evening." She gave him a cloak made of coppery dragon's scales and led him to the ballroom where the music was already in progress. The Flower Queen's daughter was there in a dress of soft rose. Her hair was as black as violets and her skin as pale as a lily. The prince was quite bedazzled and wasted no time before he asked her to dance.

"I have come to free you," he whispered in her ear as he spun her around the dance floor.

"Set me free?" the maiden asked. "What makes you think I want to be rescued?"

"Do you not?" asked the prince. "Then I shall go...."

"No, wait!" the princess said. "I do wish to leave. But they watch me so carefully!"

"Then wait for my signal!" said the prince. "When you see me leave, follow, and we shall ride away together."

Before the last dance of the evening, the prince slipped away and waited for the Flower Queen's daughter near the stables. Just before midnight she appeared. Together they leaped upon his horse and rode down the mountain as fast, aye faster, than the wind. It was not long before they reached the home of the Flower Queen.

"Thief!" screamed the dragon mother when she realized what had happened. "I trusted that human child, and he has stolen my daughter-in-law!" The dragon mother's screams woke her sleeping son, who flew into a rage when he learned what happened.

"I know just where to find her," he growled. "She has no doubt returned to her mother's palace." He flew around the tower's of the Flower Queen's palace, but she called up a bower of roses to grow as high as the highest walls. The thorns protected them well, and the dragon could not get through. In anger and disgust, he returned to his own palace.

"I wish to marry your daughter," the prince boldly told the queen.

"Then ask her," said the queen. "The choice is not mine to make."

"I will marry you," said the princess, who had fallen quite in love with the handsome prince. "But I can live with you for only six months of the year. As long as the earth is green and growing I will remain by your side. But when everything dies and returns to the ground, when the snows of winter blanket the land, I will return here to live with my mother. It is my sacred duty, and one I will not turn my back on."

"Gladly," said the prince, who would deny his beloved nothing. And that is how they spent the remainder of their days, with the princess coming and going with the seasons. In spite of the separation, they were happy with each other, and remained happy forever and always.

Snowdrop and Flame

The Sky Women were another form of the Rusalki, *spirits of the forests and waterways. During* Rusalki *Week at the beginning of summer they were believed to rise from the waters and dance. Festivals were held in their honor, and people believed that where the* Rusalki *danced the grass grew thick and crops were more abundant. The first snowfall of the year was also attributed to them. Slavic women would go outside and make snow women and children in honor of the Sky Women.*

Once on a time, long and long and very long ago, there lived a poor charcoal burner and his wife. They had a tiny cottage high in the mountains with plenty to eat and drink. Their only sorrow in the world was that they had no children.

Secretly, the wife prayed to the Sky Women. In winter, when the snows were deep, she formed a little girl out of the ice and snow and said, "If only I could have such a fine daughter!" She felt a cool wind caress her face and knew that the sky maidens had heard her plea.

Shortly after midwinter, on a chilly and beautiful day, the couple stood outside their cottage and gazed at the icy peaks around their home. A myriad of icicles hung from the roof as thick as lace, and the woman sighed. "If only we were blessed with as many children as there are icicles on our roof."

"If only we were blessed with one," returned her husband.

There was a sharp crack above their heads. Just as the wife looked up, a tiny icicle fell from the gable and dropped into her open mouth. She swallowed it, and felt a warmth spreading through her stomach. "Perhaps our prayers have been answered," she said. "Perhaps I will soon give birth to a snow child."

"What strange ideas you have!" laughed her husband. "As if such a thing could be!"

In late autumn of that year, the wife gave birth to a little girl who was as white as snow and as cold as ice. If they placed her in the crib near the fire she would howl and scream. She was only happy when she lay near the door, not seeming to mind the draft that blew in.

The girl grew quickly, as only faerie children do, and by the solstice she could walk and speak. Her parents knew she was enchanted, but they loved her despite her strange ways. What did it matter if she wished to spend the hot summer months living in the root cellar? Did it really trouble anyone else when she slept outside in winter with snow drifts for her blanket and blocks of ice for her pillow? While her parents sat shivering by the fire, she would be dancing in a snowstorm.

One particularly chilling winter the mother sighed and said, "By the blessed maidens, as much as I love our little Snowdrop, I wish I had given birth to a fire son! Then we would be able to spend more time with our child!"

No sooner had the words left her mouth than a big spark from the roaring fire leaped upon her lap, singeing the wool that covered her

stomach. "Ah!" she laughed, "perhaps the Sky Maidens will send me the fire son I desire!"

Her husband knew better than to laugh at his wife this time. Shortly after the summer solstice the wife gave birth to a son with rosy cheeks and flaming red hair. He screamed mightily until they placed his crib near the fire. Only there would he sleep soundly. Nor would he let his sister, with her ice-cold touch, come anywhere near him. She, on her part, stayed as far away from her brother as was possible. "He burns!" she'd complain, rubbing the welts raised by his fiery touch.

The couple loved their little Flame, but he was no easier to raise than his sister had been. He grew quickly, as only the faerie children do, and before the seasons had completed a single turning he was able to run outside and talk and play. His family grew accustomed to his strange ways. If he never left the hearth in winter, what of it? If he spent the summer months sunning himself like a great lizard, who was there to complain? The only problem was that neither brother nor sister could stand to be near the other.

Snowdrop grew into a beautiful maiden, and Flame as handsome a youth as any at a country dance. And suddenly, they found themselves very much alone. Their parents fell ill to a wasting disease, and coughed their spirits up to heaven.

"Whatever shall we do?" wept Snowdrop.

"I do not know about you, Sister, but I intend to set out into the world to seek my fortune," replied Flame.

"Then I shall go with you," said his sister. "Two shortens the road, they say."

"How can that be?" protested her brother. "As much as I love you, my sister, we cannot be in the same place. You nearly freeze me through just by standing there, and I always leave burns on your fair skin if you come too close."

"I wouldn't worry so much if I were you, Dear Brother. Mother had long been teaching me the old ways, and I have discovered many a secret myself. I have made each of us a cloak spun of spider's silk and woven under the light of the full moon. It shall keep you quite warm in my presence, and I in turn shall not burn in yours."

"Brilliant! Then let us be on our way." And for the first time in all their brief lives, they were able to walk down the path arm-in-arm.

For a year they traveled through mountain and village visiting the great cities of Gdansk and Warsaw and Krakow. When they grew weary of traveling, they built for themselves a fine hut, where they lived quite happily and simply.

Happiness in this world is often short-lived, and their solitude was broken one spring day by a nobleman and his band of hunters. He caught sight of the beautiful Snowdrop dancing in the chill mountain air in nothing but her shift. "Who can this beautiful maiden be?" he whispered to his men. "Why has she kept herself hidden in this wilderness?"

To the maiden he called, "Beautiful One? Who are you? Surely not one of the terrible *Wilas*, who drive men's heart's to distraction?" The sweet maiden said her name was Snowdrop, and she told the gathered men that while her brother could not stand the cold, she could not stand the heat.

"Will you be my wife?" the nobleman asked, caring little for her strange history, only knowing that he loved her dearly.

"I will," she said. "My only request is that we take my brother, too." The nobleman built her a castle made of ice deep in the caves beneath the mountains so that it would never melt. For his new brother-in-law he built a second castle with a great fireplace in every room. Even the coldest winds of January would not chill its inhabitants.

At the birth of their first child, Snowdrop and her husband hosted a grand feast, and asked the handsome Flame to attend. The red-haired youth did not appear till everyone had sat down to the tables, and when he did they began to fall over each other in their haste to get outside. "It's too hot in here!" they complained. "No one can be in the same room with him and not get burned."

The nobleman grew suddenly angry so that his face was nearly as red as Flame's. "If I had known you would ruin my party, I never would have invited you!" he snapped.

Flame could only laugh. "You can't get angry over this, my dear brother-in-law. Neither my sister nor I can control our nature. As much as she loves the cold, I love the heat."

"Get out of my home!" the nobleman screamed. "I do not want you visiting your sister again. Do not think to return to your castle for it is really mine, and I no longer wish to give you shelter. Go! Do not let me see your ugly face again."

Flame considered the nobleman's words a moment, and then he suddenly smiled. "I will go," he said, "but first let us embrace and part as brothers." Before the nobleman could answer, he found himself caught tight in Flame's embrace. He struggled to free himself, but it was no use. The searing agony left him screaming, and by the time Snowdrop reached them he lay dead on the ground, nothing but a charred cinder.

"What...have...you...done?" she said slowly. "What have you done?"

"He was a boor, Sister, you're better off," said Flame.

"He was my husband, and I loved him!" With these words, Snowdrop flew at her brother, nails outstretched to claw his face. Such a fight was never seen in all the lands of the earth! It ended as only it could end, with Snowdrop melting into a puddle of water and Flame crumbling into a smoking cinder. And so ended the brief lives of the snow daughter and fire son.

And Snowdrop's baby? When nothing remained of the mother, three beautiful maidens descended from the heavens and took the sleeping child from its cradle. They returned to the sky, to raise the girl as one of their own. Sometimes, after a storm, if you are lucky, you will see her. She is the multi-colored rainbow.

The Legend of the North Wind

There is an old Slavic curse which goes something like this, "On the sea, on the ocean, on a far distant isle, live three brothers, the Winds. One is the North, the second is the East, the third is the West. Blow, strong winds, blow heartache and sadness into the heart of (an unrequited love) so that she may think of nothing but me for all the days of her life." This gives rise to the fact that the ancient Slavs believed in elemental gods. Svarog *was the god of the sky, and his childen were* Dazhbog *(the sun) and* Svarogich *(fire). In folklore many of these elementals have come down to us as faeries: the spirits of the seasons, of weather, and of field and forest. In this tale, the ancient God of Storms has become a "Jack Frost" kind of figure, one who handsomely rewards those who honor him and cruelly punishes those who fail to recognize his power.*

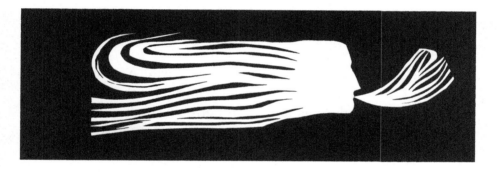

There was once upon a time a peasant woman who had a daughter named Kasienka and a stepdaughter named Inek. Kasienka had her own way in everything, and whatever she did was right in her mother's eyes. But Inek had a hard time. Let her do what she would, she was always blamed, and got small thanks for all the trouble she took. Nothing was right, everything was wrong. Yet if the truth were known, the girl was worth her weight in gold — so unselfish and goodhearted was she.

Still, the stepmother did not like her, and poor Inek's days were spent in weeping for it was impossible to live peacefully with the woman. The wicked woman was determined to get rid of the girl by fair means or foul, and kept saying to her husband, "Send her away, Old Man. Send her away. Send her anywhere, I care not. Just send her away so that my eyes will never again be plagued by the sight of her or my ears tormented with the sound of her voice. Send her out into the fields, and if the *polewiki** do not get her then the North Wind will."

In vain did the poor old father weep and implore her pity, but he was a weak-willed man, afraid to be alone. He knew he had married a witch, and dared not say her nay. So he placed his daughter in a sled, not even daring to give her a blanket to keep herself warm, and drove her out onto the bare, open fields. There he kissed her and left her, driving home as fast as he could that he might not witness her miserable death.

Deserted by her father, the poor girl sat down under a rowan tree at the edge of the forest and began to weep silently. Suddenly she heard a faint sound. It was the North Wind running through the forest, cracking his fingers and whistling a chilly tune as he went. At length he reached the rowan tree beneath which she was sitting, and with a crisp crackling sound he landed beside her and looked at her lovely face.

"Well?" he snapped when she did not say anything. "Do you know who I am? I am the North Wind, King of Winter. I am the one who turns the rivers to ice and the ground to rock. I drive the birds southward with my piercing winds and send the bears to their caves. I am Cold and Death. And I am your death, little one."

"Greetings to you, Mighty King," the girl sniffed. "So you have come to chill my bones?"

The North Wind cocked his head to one side and asked, "Are you warm?"

"I'm quite warm, my lord," she said, although her shivering betrayed her.

Then the King of Winter bent over the girl, and the crackling sound grew louder, and the air seemed to be full of knives and darts. Again he asked, "Maiden, are you warm? Are you warm, my lovely child?"

Though her breath was almost frozen on her lips, she whispered as

*The *polewiki* are spirits of the fields, from the Polish word *pole,* meaning field. It was from this that Poland took its name.

bravely as she could, "I am quite toasty, my lord. Almost too warm, if truth be told."

The North Wind gnashed his teeth. He cracked his fingers. The winds around them howled louder than ever, and for the last time he asked her, "Maiden, are you still warm? Are you still warm, Little Dove?"

The poor girl was so stiff and numb that she could barely gasp, "Oh yes, my lord, I'm still warm. It is kind of you to ask."

Now her gentle, courteous words and her uncomplaining ways melted the heart of the Winter Lord, and he took pity on her. He wrapped her up in furs and covered her with blankets, and he fetched a great box in which were beautiful jewels and a rich robe embroidered in gold and silver. And she put the robe on and looked more lovely than ever. Then the North Wind stepped with her into his sled pulled by six silvery horses, and took her to his castle. "I have a warm fire going for guests such as yourself," he said kindly. "We will thaw your bones, and then I will take you home."

In the meantime the cruel witch was waiting at home for news of her stepdaughter's death. She hummed happily to herself, preparing pancakes for the funeral feast. She said to her husband, "Old fool, you had better go out into the fields and find your daughter's body and bring her home for burial."

"Yes my love," he said sadly, bundling himself in his heavy coat and wrapping a scarf around his head.

Just as the old man was leaving the house the little dog under the table began to bark, saying, "Your daughter shall live to be your delight, her daughter shall die this very night."

"Evil beast!" the woman kicked the dog. "Hold your lying tongue. For this I conjured for you the power of speech? Stop it!" The dog only stared at her with large, knowing eyes and the old witch shivered. "I will give you a pancake," she said, quickly changing her tune. "But you must say, 'Her daughter shall have much silver and gold; his daughter is frozen quite stiff and cold.'"

The dog ate up the pancake, wagging his tail at the treat, and when he was done said, "His daughter shall wear a crown on her head; her daughter shall die unwooed, unwed."

The old witch tried to coax the dog with more pancakes. When that did not work, she tried to terrify it with blows to his head. But he barked on, always repeating the same words. And suddenly the door creaked and flew open, and a great heavy chest was pushed in, and behind it came the stepdaughter, radiant and beautiful, in a dress all glittering with silver and gold. For a moment the stepmother's eyes were dazzled.

"Where did you get these riches?" she snapped.

"From the King of Winter," said Inek. "He is really quite kind once you get to know him."

The witch called to her husband. "Old fool, yoke the horses at once onto the sled, and take my daughter to the same field and leave her on the same spot. The same spot exactly! What's due will surely come to her."

So the old man took the girl and left her beneath the same tree where he had parted from his daughter. In a few minutes the North Wind came past and, looking at the girl, he said, "Are you warm, maiden?"

"What?" she snapped. "Are you as blind as you are ugly? Of course, I am not warm! I'm freezing! Who wouldn't be? It's winter and that cursed mother of mine has sent me out into a blizzard."

This angered the North Wind greatly, and he cracked his fingers and gnashed his teeth, and froze her to death where she sat. Such is the end for rude young maidens!

In the cottage her mother was waiting for her return. The longer the girl was gone, the more impatient she grew, and she snapped to her husband. "Why are you standing there? Get out the sled and fetch her home. The chest she has is probably too large to carry alone."

"Your daughter is frozen quite stiff and cold," interrupted the little dog from his place near the fire. "She shall never have a chest full of gold."

"Wicked, wicked beast!" screamed the woman. "How dare you tell such lies! I will give you a hot pancake if only you'd say...." She never got to finish her sentence. At that moment the door blew in and before them all stood the Winter King.

"Mother, are you cold?" he smiled bitterly, and clasped her in his embrace. The evil mother died almost instantly, a look of horror frozen on her face.

The Death of the Sun Lord

The pagan Slavs personified the sky as the Svarog, *whose son was named* Dazhbog, *which literally means "the Sun." According to most tales,* Dazhbog *lived in a golden palace in the east. Each morning he drove forth in his diamond-studded chariot which was drawn by twelve white horses with fiery manes. He is believed to be the father of the* Zorya, *the sisters of fate. Later myths describe* Dazhbog *as a handsome knight dressed in gold armor. In the following tale are found many traditional mythical elements — including the "tree of knowledge" which bears the apples of immortality.*

Many, many thousands of years ago there lived a mighty king named *Svarog* who was blessed with a clever and handsome son named *Dahzbog*. When he was only ten years old, the boy was smarter than all the king's counsellors put together, and when he was twenty he was the greatest hero in the whole kingdom. His father could not make enough of his son, and always had him clothed in golden clothes which shone and sparkled like the sun. His mother gave him a white horse, which never slept and which flew like the wind. All the people in the land loved him dearly and called him the Sun Lord, for they did not think his like existed under the sun.

Now it happened one night that both his parents had the same extraordinary dream. They dreamt that a girl all dressed in red had come to them and said, "If you wish that your son should really become the Sun Lord, let him go out into the world and search for the Tree of the Sun. When he has found it, let him pluck a golden apple from it and bring it home."

When the king and queen had each related their dreams to the other, they were much amazed that they should each have dreamed exactly the same thing. The king said to his wife, "This is clearly a sign from heaven that we should send our son out into the world in order that he may come home the great Sun Lord, as the Red Girl said, not only in name but in deed."

The queen consented, although she wept as any mother would, and the king at once bade his son set forth in search of the Tree of the Sun, from which he was to pluck a golden apple. *Dahzbog* was delighted at the prospect, and set out on his travels that very day. For a long time he wandered all through the world, and it was not till the ninety-ninth day after he started that he found an old man who was able to tell him where the Tree of the Sun grew.

He followed his directions and rode on his way, and after another ninety-nine days, he arrived at a golden castle which stood in the middle of a vast wilderness. He knocked at the door, which was opened noiselessly and by invisible hands. Finding no one about, the prince rode on, and came to a great meadow where the Sun Tree grew.

When he reached the tree he put out his hand to pick a golden apple, but all of a sudden the tree grew higher so that he could not reach its fruit. Then he heard someone behind him laughing. Turning round, he saw the girl in red walking towards him, who addressed him in these words, "Do you really imagine, brave son of the earth, that you can pluck an apple so easily from the Tree of the Sun? Before you can do that, you have a difficult task before you. You must guard the tree for nine days and nine nights from the ravages of two wild black wolves, who will try to harm it. Do you think you can undertake this?"

"Yes," answered the Sun Lord. "I will guard the Tree of the Sun nine days and nine nights."

Then the girl continued, "Remember, though, if you do not succeed the Sun will kill you. Now begin your watch." With these words the Red Girl went back into the golden castle. She had hardly left him when the two black wolves appeared. But the Sun Lord beat them off with his sword, and they retired, only to reappear in a very short time. The Sun Lord chased them away once more, but he had hardly sat down to rest when the two black wolves were on the scene again.

This went on for seven days and nights, when the white horse, who had never done such a thing before, turned to the Sun Lord and said in a human voice, "Listen to what I am going to say. A *Rusalki* gave me to your mother in order that I might be of service to you. Let me warn you that if you go to sleep and let the wolves harm the tree, the Sun will surely kill you. The *Rusalki*, foreseeing this, put everyone in the world under a spell which prevents their obeying the Sun's command to take your life. But all the same, she has forgotten one person, who will certainly kill you if you fall asleep and let the wolves damage the tree. So watch and keep the wolves away."

"Who is this one creature unaffected by the spell?"

"This I know not," said the horse. "You must discover it for yourself."

Then the Sun Lord strove with all his might and kept the black wolves at bay, and conquered his desire to sleep. But on the eighth night his strength failed him, and he fell fast asleep. When he awoke a woman in black stood beside him, who said, "You have fulfilled your task very badly for you have let the two black wolves damage the Tree of the Sun. I am the mother of the Sun, and I command you to ride away from here at once, and I pronounce sentence of death upon you for you proudly let yourself be called the Sun Lord without having done anything to deserve the name." The youth mounted his horse sadly and rode home.

The people all thronged round him on his return, anxious to hear his adventures, but he told them nothing, and only to his mother did he confide what had befallen him. But the old queen laughed, and said to her son, "Don't worry, my child. You see, the *Rusalki* has protected you so far, and the Sun has found no one to kill you. So cheer up and be happy."

After a time the prince forgot all about his adventure and married a clever maiden with whom he lived very happily for some time. But one day when he was out hunting, he felt very thirsty. Coming to a stream, he stooped down to drink from it, and this caused his death, for a crab came swimming up and with its claws tore out his tongue. He was carried home in a dying condition, and as he lay on his deathbed the woman in black appeared and said, "So the Sun has, after all, found someone who was not under the *Rusalki's* spell, who has caused your death. And a similar fate will overtake everyone under the Sun who wrongfully assumes a title to which he has no right."

The Dragon of Wawel

There is a cave at the base of Wawel Castle in Krakow once said to be the home of a fierce and terrifying dragon. There is now a monument of this dragon in front of the cave, and every night fire is said to issue from his mouth.

Krakus grew up in a small farming community where the people were happy, and their bellies were always full. But he heard of the troubles that came from Wawel Hill. In a cave beneath the hill there lived a fierce dragon, a monster that ravaged the countryside, eating up the cows and sheep and goats unlucky enough to stray from the herd. And once a week, this dragon demanded an innocent young maiden for his supper.

The bravest knights in the land sought to overcome the dragon, and they all died as young men do, some foolishly and some well. No one was able to slay the dragon.

In desperation the king announced that whoever could slay the dragon would marry his daughter and rule the land after him. Many knights from far distant shores came to Wawel Hill to kill the demon beast, but they died as well, scorched by the dragon's fiery breath.

Although he was but a farmer, a tiller of the earth, Krakus had dreams of becoming a great hero. Ignoring the warnings of his family and friends, he traveled to Wawel Hill to challenge the dragon himself.

He brought with him his fattest, most delicious-looking ram, and he filled the poor creature's stomach with a mixture of straw, sulphur, and tar. Then he left the tempting morsel outside the dragon's cave.

The winged serpent was so hungry that he swallowed the animal whole, not even bothering to chew it. Soon the mixture began to burn, and smoke issued out of the dragon's ears. In terrible pain, the dragon flew to the banks of the Wisla and drank deep of the cooling waters. The water seemed only to make it worse, but the dragon drank on and on. He gulped down so much water that he could hardly move. Krakus, seeing his chance, jumped on the back of the great lizard and cut off its head with a scythe.

The farmer married the king's daughter, and when the old king died he ruled the land surrounding Wawel Hill. The city he rescued eventually took on his name, and bears it to this very day — Krakow.

The Plague

In Polish folklore, Death is personified as Marzanna, *a beautiful maiden dressed in white. Every spring the* Marzanna *was drowned or burned in effigy to celebrate the end of the death season and the return of life. She was sometimes blamed for the plague, which raged through Eastern Europe long after it had disappeared in the West.*

Marzanna, who carried the plague with her, once traveled in a boat down the Vistula to reach the city of Warsaw, which had previously escaped her ravages. She stepped ashore and walked up the main street. Her long black hair flowed down her back, and a gentle breeze swirled her skirts about her tiny, white feet. She was very beautiful, but those who knew her for what she was quickly turned their eyes away. To look her in the face would be to ask for doom.

Those who were unfortunate enough to gaze upon her blushing complexion or who paused to look at her emerald green eyes would feel as if a fist had clenched their heart. Unable to speak a word, they returned to their homes, bringing the plague with them.

The plague mistress reached the end of the high road and turned toward a small peasant dwelling. She stood in the doorway, blinking about her in the dimly lit interior.

"Who's there?" called a voice from a corner.

"A traveler," said *Marzanna*, stepping closer into the room.

"Then in God's name I bid you welcome. I am but a poor, blind woman, and few come to visit me. Sit at the hearth and warm yourself."

Marzanna stared at the woman whose sightless eyes gazed toward the door. "No one has ever welcomed me before," she said. "And for that I will spare you and the remainder of the city." Without another word the beautiful figure of Death returned to her boat and paddled down the river, changing the course of her path of destruction.

The Wolf and the Devil

In Polish mythology the wolf is often seen as a creature of good will and not something to be feared. Perhaps this comes from a pre-Christian time when the pagan moon goddess would appear in the form of a wolf. Today, wolves' teeth are a popular design on pisanki *eggs, and are considered elements of luck or wisdom.*

Zofia was walking home from the market with an apron full of cabbages for her mother. The village was far from their cabin in the forest, and the maiden paused to rest in a grove of evergreens.

Leaning against the tree, she was surprised to feel something moving about in her apron. "Whatever is that?" she whispered to herself, more curious than afraid. She was just about to dump the cabbages onto the ground when she felt a tug on the back of her skirt. She looked down to see a white wolf standing beside her. He looked up at her with yellow eyes and bared his teeth in a snarl. Before Zofia could draw breath to scream, a large and fearsome rat leaped from her apron and took off in the undergrowth. The wolf gave chase and the two quickly disappeared in the darkening woods.

Zofia hurried home after that. *"Babci!"* she called to her old grandmother who sat by the hearth shelling peas. "It's a strange tale I have for the telling!" And she told the old woman about the rat and the wolf.

"You're lucky that wolf came along when it did, my child," said the grandmother. "That rat was the devil in disguise, no doubt there to do you some mischief!"

Ever after Zofia kept an eye out for the white wolf, but it was never seen again. Nor was she ever plagued by the devil's cruel pranks.

The Sinner's Hand

This story was told to me by Dorota, a woman who cleaned my house years ago when I was living in Chicago. She said the woman involved was "a friend of a friend" in the village where she once lived. It is a common Polish folktale, found in numerous versions, and is actually quite old. I include it here to show that folklore traditions are alive and well, even in the twenty-first century.

Marta was a cruel and selfish creature. She would disobey the nuns at school, shove her little brother when she thought no one was looking, and steal money from her older sister's purse. And if she didn't get her own way, she would slap her mother. Now what kind of child would do that?

It was with some small sense of relief when Marta accidently drowned in the creek near the edge of the village. There were not many who attended the funeral of the little girl, just the priest and the poor mother. Even her own siblings refused to come.

Imagine the mother's horror when she visited the grave the next day to find that Marta's hand had risen to the surface and was sticking straight out of the ground. Dirt clung beneath the fingernails as if they had clawed their way out of the grave. It was the very same hand with which the girl had struck the mother.

Not knowing what else to do, the terrifed woman went to the village priest.

"You never punished Marta when she was bad, did you?" the priest asked, not unkindly.

"N…no," said the woman. "I was too afraid of what she would do to me then."

"The very ground of the churchyard refuses to contain your daughter, and unless you punish her now, she will continue to rise from the grave."

So with the priest there to help, the woman took a stout cane to the churchyard and beat the hand with it. As amazing as it is true, the hand returned to the earth. In the morning the ground over the grave appeared undisturbed, and a blanket of lush green grass grew over it.

The Amber Palace

Amber is a yellowish-gold, fossilized tree resin that is known for its electrical properties. It has been highly prized since ancient times and worn as both jewelry and as a talisman against evil. The ancient Poles once worshipped a sea goddess known as Jurata, *who lived in an amber palace in the Baltic Sea. Later folktales describe* Jurata *as queen of the faeries.*

In times long past there were enchanted cities that thrived beneath the stormy waters of the Baltic. And in the midst of one of these great cities rose the amber palace of *Jurata*, Queen of the Sea.

Jurata was very beautiful, indeed, with long red-gold hair and eyes as blue as sapphires. She often dressed in a gown of turquoise, decorated with pearls and the silvery scales of fishes. But it was for her wisdom and kindness that her people loved her. She ruled her kingdom justly with such compassion and understanding that even the smallest of her subjects lived without fear.

Imagine, if you can, the sea queen's anger when she heard tell of a fisherman seen casting his net near her sacred waters. She rose to the surface in her golden amber boat, intent on dragging the fisherman to his doom. "How dare he violate my laws!" she fumed. "He will be sorely punished for harming my beloved people!"

Whatever harsh words *Jurata* planned to say died on her lips when she caught sight of the man. He was handsome, as human men sometimes are, with hair as black as jet and bright blue eyes that gazed upon the sea maiden with admiration and love. A smile broke across his tan and weather-beaten face, and he said, "To what do I owe the pleasure of your visit, my queen?"

"I have come to woo you, brave fisherman, and take you for my own." From that day on, *Jurata* would rise to the surface in her amber boat to pass the evening hours with her true love.

Not everyone was happy for the devoted couple. *Piorun*, God of Thunder and Flood, burned with jealous rage when he gazed down at

Jurata and her lover. He had always fancied the sea queen as his own, and if he could not have her he would allow no one — neither god nor mortal — to lay claim to her.

From his lofty home in the clouds, he raised a mighty storm over the Baltic. Rain fell heavy and fast and the winds tossed up waves high, aye higher than the tallest towers of *Jurata's* beloved city. Many ships were destroyed in that storm, and many innocent lives were lost. *Piorun* cast thunderbolt after thunderbolt into the crashing waves, striking the sea queen in her heart, killing all her courtiers and destroying the beautiful amber palace.

His wrath not slacked, *Piorun* captured the handsome fisherman and chained him to the bottom of the sea where he has remained ever since. To this day, when there is a storm raging over the Baltic, you can sometimes hear the groans and cries of the fisherman. The amber bits, cast upon the shores by the thundering waves, are all that remain of *Jurata's* amber palace. If you are lucky enough to find one of these amber fragments, keep it with you always, as a reminder of the lost queen and her love of a human.

The Night Mare of Swinoujsie

Sometime during the fourteenth century Pope Calixtus III decreed that "no more religious rites would be held in the cave with the horse pictures," evidence that pagan horse-worship was still prevalent into the Middle Ages. The Mother-Goddess-as-Horse was well-known to the Slavs, although later folklore spoke of her as a volva, *a witch who could transform herself into a horse. "Night Mares" became creatures of evil, witches or enchantresses who would visit sleepers in the form of a horse and bring them bad dreams.*

Patek and Nikodem were lucky enough to work for the richest farmer in the village. Each evening, after a hard day's work, they were given a hearty meal of bread and sausage — and on Sunday there were even currant-filled pastries for dessert! They slept in the loft of the barn, and each had a thick straw mattress and a warm wool blanket. They would have been perfectly happy with their lot in life if it were not for the fact that Nikodem was troubled each night by a *mahrt*.

Hardly an evening went by when she did not slip through the keyhole and into Nikodem's dreams. He would wake up, pale and sweating, his heart thundering in his ears. "Patek! Patek!" he'd cry. "Stop the demon before she gets away!" But it was no use. All that remained of the night mare were hoofmarks in the dust.

"Tonight I will stay awake," said Patek, "and when the *mahrt* sneaks into the room I will plug up the keyhole." And so he did. Patek watched in silence as the *mahrt* slipped through the keyhole in the form of a mist. He watched as his poor, tormented friend tossed and turned beneath his blanket and…he…slowly…crept across the room to plug up the keyhole with a bit of wax.

"We have her now!" he shouted. "Nikodem, wake up!"

As Nikodem awoke, the mist in the room materialized into a beautiful maiden. Both men felt love grow in their hearts, and they fell to quarreling over which of them should marry the girl.

"She has already chosen me," said Nikodem. "It is my dreams that she has troubled."

"Obviously she should belong to me. I was the one who plugged up the keyhole," insisted Patek. "If it weren't for me, we would not even be having this conversation!"

"If anyone cares to ask my opinion," the maiden interrupted, "I would be glad to give it."

"I will listen," said Patek.

"Please tell us your decision," said Nikodem.

"I love you both dearly," smiled the maiden most winningly, "but I cannot choose. Let me go and ask my father, the King of Dreams, to decide for me. Only…you will have to unplug the keyhole first."

"Gladly!" said both men, stumbling over one another in their haste to reach the door first. But when they removed the wax the *marht* gave a whinney of triumph and slipped out through the keyhole. Neither of the hired men ever saw the beautiful maiden again, nor were they ever plagued by bad dreams.

The She-Wolf

The She-Wolf is a very old form of the Mother Earth Goddess once worshipped throughout Europe. Slavic tribes would pass a newborn child through a wolf skin, saying that it was "born of the She-Wolf." The practice remained for several centuries after the coming of Christianity as a supposed "protection against witches," although it was more than likely a continuation of the old wolf cult. Later Polish myth, influenced by the Church, said that She-Wolves were witches that could transform themselves into beasts.

On the banks of the Wistua, near a village without a name, there stood an abandoned mill. Nobody would go near the mill because it was the home of a She-Wolf, a fierce and frightening creature.

A soldier was traveling up the river on his way home from the wars when he spied the old mill. The sky above was grey and looming, threatening rain at any moment. "There is no one here to tell me no," he said to his horse, "so I think we will spend the night here." He brought his horse inside and made a fire in the parlor. Then he carried his bedroll up to the loft above.

Shortly after midnight there was a scratching sound out front and the door crashed in. It was the She-Wolf and she was in a foul mood. The hunt had not gone well and she was very, very hungry. She was surprised for but a moment when she spied the horse. Then she lept upon it and devoured it all. The soldier watched from above, careful not to say a word.

When the She-Wolf was finished, she stretched before the fire, sniffing around it curiously. She knew that someone had been here, but she did not think of looking up into the loft. Who would be foolish enough to stay in a haunted mill? She let out a long, mournful howl and then growled between sharp teeth, "Skin off! Skin off!" The She-Wolf raised herself onto her hind legs, and the soldier watched as the wolf hide seemed to slide right off the beast. Where the wolf had been, a beautiful maiden now stood, naked in the glow of the fire. She wrapped herself in a robe and hung the wolf skin in its place on a peg near the fire. Then the maiden yawned and stretched before settling by the fire to sleep.

The soldier crept quietly down from the loft. Carefully, so as not to disturb the sleeping witch, he picked up the wolf skin and hid it in his traveling bag. Then he leaned over the maiden and gently shook her shoulder. "Time to get up, Witch, and meet your new husband."

The maiden snarled when she saw the strange man standing in the middle of her home. "Skin on!" she shouted, but it was no use. The soldier now had possession of the wolf pelt.

"I will one day give you back your skin," said the soldier, "but only after you have proved yourself to be a good wife."

"You leave me little choice," snapped the witch. "But I will have my revenge." And so the couple lived as man and wife, and had two children.

The boys grew into handsome young lads, and as young boys always are, they were very curious. One day they were searching through their father's possessions when they found the wolf skin. They ran to the shed where the soldier was working. "Father, Father!" said the eldest. "Tell us about the wolf you killed."

"How do you know of that?" asked the father.

"We found the wolf pelt in the chest you always keep locked," said the second son. "Only…this time it wasn't locked."

"Your mother was once a wolf," said the soldier truthfully, "but I have kept her wolf skin and she has made a fine mother. I think she is happier this way."

"Then you think wrong, Husband," his wife spoke quietly from the door. "Once I roamed free under the light of the full moon, and reveled in the joy of the hunt. You have kept me prisoner all of these years."

"And what of it?" asked the soldier smugly. "What can you do about it now?"

"Plenty," said the witch, slamming shut the door of the shed. She drew across the bolt and locked it securely, imprisoning her sons as well as her husband. Then she returned to the mill where she found her skin hidden away in the unlocked chest. Sighing happily, she whispered, "Skin on! Skin on!" The wolf pelt crept up her limbs, merging with her flesh, and where the woman once stood there now stood a wolf. The wolf's lips pulled back in a grimace of satisfaction. She threw back her head and howled out her joy before running into the woods, never to be seen near the mill again.

And her husband and sons? Perhaps they were able to escape, perhaps not. But the She-Wolf cared little for that.

The Red Bird

Beyond the seven seas, and beyond their furthest shores, there lived a man named Jedrek who was a hunter. What did he hunt, you ask? He did not hunt for bear, or wild boar, or for the great wolf; he did not seek the fish in the stream or the flocks that passed through each spring and autumn. He did not make sport of the elk, the deer or the moose. What he hunted for was a tiny red bird, just one. And he spent seven years doing that.

Jedrek had a wife and daughter. They all lived in the middle of a great forest, far from town or village. Each morning the wife went out into the woods to gather herbs, and one day she was struck down dead by a flash of summer lightning. Jedrek buried her, and mourned her, and after a while he left his daughter to tend the cottage while he once again pursued the tiny red bird. Hunting the red bird was all he knew. It had become his obsession, his life.

One morning when his daughter was fetching water at the stream, a wolf attacked and devoured her. Jedrek found what was left of her body. He buried her near her mother, mourned her a spell, and after a while he took up his rifle and went in search of the elusive red bird. Hunting the bird was his passion.

One winter while crossing the ice Jedrek fell through a weak spot and was drowned. Springtime floods washed his body ashore. There was no one to bury him. Crows and ravens and other carrion birds feasted on his corpse. Ants and beetles and bottle flies finished the rest. By summer, all that remained were Jedrek's bones, picked clean and bleached white.

As the leaves of the forest took on their autumn cast, the red bird flew down from its mountain home. It spied the bones sitting in their leafy nest and paused to take a closer look. It landed on Jedrek's skeletal hand. Suddenly the bony fingers closed over the little red bird and held it tight in a fist of death. "You have hunted me all your life!" chirped the bird in sorrow. "And now you hunt me in death. And for what? What use am I to you now?"

But there was no answer from Jedrek. Both bird and man were dead, and no one was left to bury them.

The Two Corpses

Czestochowa is a village in southern Poland. In one of its churches is a painting of the Madonna and Child, and because the faces in the painting are very dark the Lady is known as the Black Madonna. The painting was supposedly done by St. Luke, and many are the miracles attributed to it.

After many years of faithful service in the army, a soldier named Ladislaus was on his way home to the city of Czestochowa. His first stop was to pray at the shrine of Our Lady of Czestochowa, the Black Virgin. Then he made his way to the farm of his parents, who lived a short distance out of town.

The sun had set many hours before, but he was not afraid. He had walked this road a thousand times in his youth and could, no doubt, walk it blindfolded. As he made his way past the graveyard, where all his ancestors were buried, he heard a voice call out to him, "You, there! Wait!"

Ladislaus looked back and saw a corpse running towards him with its skin falling off in chunks and its eyes hanging from the sockets. "There is no escape!" the corpse cried, spilling teeth as it shouted. "You are mine!"

The soldier was no fool. There was nothing that would induce him to stay. He glanced around and caught sight of a tiny church at the edge of the graveyard. Running as fast as he could to reach it, he tore open the door, slamming it shut behind him.

Although there was no one in sight, Ladislaus saw several candles burning near the altar. Beneath the tapers lay a coffin with another corpse stretched out. "Better not risk it," the soldier thought, crossing himself piously and hiding away in the confessional. It was not a moment too soon. The corpse from the road ripped the door to the church off its hinges and rushed in. "You cannot hide from me!" he cried. "Not even in here!"

"Who disturbs my peace?" said a voice from the coffin.

"I've followed a soldier here," said the first corpse, "and now I will make him my dinner!"

"Not here you won't," said the second corpse, sitting up in his coffin.

"He is in my church now, therefore he is mine."

"Oh, no, he's not!"

"Oh, yes, he is!"

As the soldier watched from his hiding place, the second corpse leaped from his coffin and sank his teeth into the first. A fight ensued and the soldier quaked in fear because he knew that whichever one was left standing would feast on his bones. "Oh, Blessed Lady of Czestochowa, protect this poor sinner!" he cried.

From outside a cock crowed. Dawn crept slowly across the floor of the church, and when the sunlight reached the two corpses, they both fell to the ground, as lifeless as they should be.

Such is the power of the Blessed Lady.

The Flaming Castle

In the Tatra Mountains, high above field and stream, there stands an old castle made of stone. No one lives in the castle, but each night a fire is seen to burn hotly, and the flames are so high that they rise up over the walls and may be seen far and wide, painting the sky an angry red.

An old man in want of firewood climbed up the mountain's path, gathering fallen twigs and branches as he went. Eventually he reached the great iron doors of the castle. Curiosity got the better of him. "All my life I have heard strange tales of this castle," he whispered to himself, "and now I will find out the truth of the matter. What harm can come to me while the sun shines?"

He pushed at the doors and they opened with a groan. He wandered through the neglected courtyard and entered the great hall. And there, much to his surprise, he saw an assembly of noblemen and their ladies sitting down to a feast. There were musicians and entertainers playing in the corner and plenty of servants bobbing and weaving between the tables, serving up food and wine.

"You there," said one of the servants, drawing the old man aside, "this is for you." And he placed in the old man's coat pocket a gold coin.

"What's this?" asked the old man, but when he looked up the servant, in fact the entire assembly, had vanished. He shivered, for the room had grown suddenly chilled. "Could I have imagined it?" he murmured, gazing at the cold hearth and the empty, worm-eaten tables. Much confused, he made his way back out to the courtyard, now bathed in the light of the moon.

A soldier stepped directly in his path, and the old man knew that he faced a specter for the soldier carried his head under his arm. "Tell no one what you have seen," he instructed, "or great evil will befall you."

"I doubt anyone would believe me anyway," said the old man, not in the least afraid. In his eighty-five years he had seen a number of strange things.

"Now go," said the specter, and the old man, shouldering his burden, returned to the village. He glanced behind him once, and saw that the castle was engulfed in flames.

The old man kept the gold coin, telling no one of it, but his granddaughter found it while cleaning the chamber. It was not long before word reached the town council, and the old man was summoned before them.

"Where did you get this coin?" they demanded. "How can a poor old man such as yourself come by such wealth? Surely it must be stolen."

"I can't tell you," said the old man. "I was told great evil would befall me."

"Great evil will befall you if you don't tell us," one of the elders continued. "You will spend what years you have left in jail."

Thinking of his children and grandchildren, the old man sighed. "I will tell you," he said. "I have not lived this long to end my years in misery." And he told the assembled crowd what he saw at the flaming castle. He told of the nobles and their ladies, the fine fragrant food and the assembled musicians. And he told of the flames which surrounded the castle. When he had finished, a whirlwind blew into the courtroom, carrying away the old man before the startled eyes of those gathered. He was not heard from again.

For many years no one dared approach the castle. But word of the old man's misfortune spread far and wide, and it eventually brought to the village a young nobleman, a knight. "That mountaintop is the perfect spot to set up my rule," he said. "I will restore that castle to its former glory. And what of these tales I hear? Nothing but a *bajka*, a fairy tale to frighten strangers away."

The terrain being too steep for his horse, the knight set out on foot with only his servant for company. It was the middle of the night, and the sky was bathed red by the flames from the castle. "Well, the peasants spoke true, at least about the fire," the knight said. "But it is probably nothing more than a band of robbers using the castle as their home base."

"Go back!" a voice boomed down the mountain.

"W…what was that?" the servant trembled.

"Ignore it," the knight said. "It will not deter us."

Twice more the strange voice thundered through the night air. "Go back! Go back!"

They kept on, however, heedless of the warning. At last they reached the iron gates of the castle. The headless soldier blocked their path. "Who goes there!" said the head the soldier carried under his arm.

"I do," said the knight, afraid of nothing. "And you stand in my way."

"But what is your name?" the ghost insisted.

"That is none of your affair," said the knight, gesturing for his servant to give him his sword.

"As you wish," sighed the ghost, stepping aside to make way for a black knight who came storming out of the castle on his black destrier. Before the visiting nobleman could raise his sword, the horseman dragged him into the courtyard. The iron gates slammed shut behind them, and the knight was seen no more. In terror, the servant ran back to the village. Since that time, no one else has been brave enough or foolish enough to investigate too closely the flaming castle on the mountain. And there it sits to this very day, keeping close its secrets.

The Novice
and
The Peacocks

Father Janek took one of his young charges with him when he traveled to the city of Gdansk. He had raised Tomislaw since finding him on the steps of the chapel, and he loved him as if he were his own son. The trip was a reward to the boy, who had tended well his studies and diligently prayed each morning, noon and night.

Tomislaw had never seen a human soul other than the holy brothers that lived with him at the monastery. Entering through the city gates, the man and boy saw all sorts of wonders. A group of beautiful young maidens, dressed in pretty gowns with brightly colored ribbons and flowers entwined in their hair, passed close to where they stood. Tomislaw stared after them with wide-eyed wonder. "What are they, Father?" he whispered. Until that moment he had never laid eyes on a woman.

"Peacocks," snapped the old man. "Pampered, perfumed peacocks. Pay them no mind."

Tomislaw said nothing more, silently following the abbot on his errands. It was not until they reached the gates of the city that the abbot noticed his young novice was crying.

"What is it, Boy?" he asked. "What has you so upset?"

"Nothing, Father," sniffed the boy, wiping his nose on his sleeve.

"Come now, tell me now or tell me later, but tell me you will."

"It's just that…it's just that I want to take one of the peacocks home! You've let the other brothers keep pets, can't I?"

"Enough!" said the abbot, dragging poor Tomislaw away by the ear. "I'll hear no more of the matter!"

Never again did the abbot allow the boy to return to Gdansk, and never did Tomislaw forget the image of his beautiful peacocks.

The Devil's Visit

Two brothers and their wives lived together in a cottage outside of Walbrzych. Dadiwek and his wife Emilia had three children, but Edek and his wife had none. It was with envy that Fania, the childless woman, looked upon her sister-in-law. "If only I could give birth to such fine, rosy children," she sighed, "I would give almost anything."

One day, while both husbands were working in the fields, the Devil and his son knocked at the cottage door in their semblance. As bold as can be they sat down to supper. The children, however, were not fooled. They knew the demons for what they were.

"Mother," whispered the oldest of the boys, "Mother, look! Father's got long claws."

"Don't bother me with your nonsense!" she snapped, stirring the kettle over the fire. "I do not have time for this."

"But, Mother!" said the second boy. "Look, Mother, he's got a tail, too!"

"Hush!" she scolded, glancing over at the two men. "I see nothing wrong. Do you want your father to hear?"

Then the youngest piped in, "Mother, look! Father has long, iron teeth and red eyes!"

At last Emilia believed them, for her youngest child was known to never lie. She comforted them as best she could, and tried to catch the eye of her sister-in-law. But Fania would not look her way, and when the demons went outside she went with them.

"Quick, my children!" said Emilia. "Onto the stove, now!" She spread juniper twigs in front and made the sign of the cross over each of her boys.

Emilia then climbed onto the rafters for safety, taking with her a three-pronged fork. Soon the demons returned.

"The woman was delicious to eat," said one, "but I'm still hungry."

"Then we shall eat the other wife," said the second demon. "And finish the children off for dessert!"

The demons, no longer in disguise, searched the room. They could not see the children because the juniper branches cast a protective spell over them. Yet it was not long before they discovered Emilia in the rafters.

"You there!" cried the elder demon. "Come down here now. I do not want to climb up after you."

"Never!" said Emila, waving her pitchfork at them. "You will not get me without a fight!"

Just as the demons were about to climb into the rafters, a red cock crowed, and the devil cried out. "Blast it! Our time is short!"

Again they tried to climb into the rafters when a white cock crowed. The devil cried out, "We haven't but a moment more!" and scrambled to the door. Then crowed a black cock, and the devil shouted, "He's my murderer!" Both demons vanished, never to trouble Emila and her children again.

The Village Dance

There was a young girl named Lydia who grew up in the Carpathian Mountain Range. She felt the calling very early in life and wished to be a nun. She swore that nothing would sway her from her path.

Shortly after her sixteenth birthday, as she was making her preparations for the convent, one of her dear friends stopped by. "There's to be a dance tonight on the village green," said her friend.

"You know I leave for the convent on the morrow," smiled Lydia. "I cannot go to a dance."

"But this is your last night with us!" her friend insisted. "After tonight, you will no longer be allowed to attend such festivities." Reluctantly, Lydia finally agreed to go, and she allowed her friend to dress her in a gown of white and entwine white flowers in her hair.

When they arrived at the green, Lydia sat alone beneath a spreading oak, smoothing her skirts around her. It was not long before a handsome young man asked her to dance.

"You're a stranger here, I see," remarked Lydia.

"I know you better than you think," the youth replied rather mysteriously, grabbing hold of her hand and swinging her into the dance.

They danced merrily to the tune of pipe and accordion, and after awhile Lydia fell to flirting with the young stranger and even accepted a drink of punch.

"I would like to kiss you...." murmured the stranger, and Lydia let him.

He teased the maiden, toying with the crucifix that hung around her neck. "This is a silly bit of jewelry," he remarked.

"My mother gave it to me," said the girl proudly.

"You put too much faith in it," he said. "It will not protect you from the evils of the world. Why don't you take it off?"

Because she wanted to please the handsome young stranger, she took off her crucifix and left it near her belongings.

When they joined the dance again, her friend started to scream, "Lydia! Lydia! Look at his feet!"

All eyes turned to the couple on the green, and Lydia herself looked down to see that instead of feet the man had cloven hooves. All reason for pretense over, the devil dropped his disguise and stood in the midst of the crowd. Lydia then knew him for what he was, but it was too late. The ground suddenly opened up beneath them, and girl and demon were swallowed up.

The fault, of course, was all Lydia's own. The devil could never have taken her as long as she wore her cross.

The Trader and the *Psotnik*

As Romuald was traveling through the Tatra's on his way home from a trading mission, he heard a voice call out to him. "Romuald, Romuald! Where do you go? Stay awhile!"

He looked all around but could see no one. "I have spent too much time alone in the mountains," he laughed, shaking his head and reshouldering his pack. "I am beginning to hear strange voices."

"Romuald! Over here!" There was no ignoring the plea, and the trader followed the voice where it led away from the path until he found himself standing at the base of a large pine tree.

"Who's there?" he called.

"Look up, Romuald. I am trapped in a fork of branches." The man looked up and saw wedged near the trunk a tiny spirit in a glass bottle. There was a stopper stuck tight in the opening and three crosses were painted on the seal.

"Set me free, Romuald. I beg of you."

"It seems to me, little spirit, that somebody placed you there with a purpose. What mischief have you been up to?"

"I will reward you handsomely!" the spirit promised.

Romuald thought long and hard. When in the great cities he saw a number of people who were sick and dying. "If you will bestow on me the power of healing, I will set you free."

"Done," the spirit said quickly.

"I'm not done!" interrupted the trader. "I also want a potion that will turn to gold anything I sprinkle it on."

"Anything you wish," the spirit agreed, "only let me out!"

Romuald picked up the glass bottle. Gently buffing out the crosses with the sleeve of his coat, he then proceeded to pry out the stopper. Pop! the cork came flying out and the imp tumbled out to the ground.

It twisted and grew before his eyes, and soon enough there stood before the awe-struck trader a tall and dark-haired fairie lad dressed in a cloak of white and red. "I thank you for setting me free," he said. Then he removed from his cloak two small phials.

One of the phials contained a clear liquid. "This is the Water of Life," said the faerie man. "Use it to cure any disease. And with this you may turn any object into gold," he added, handing over a phial of blood red liquid.

"Thank you," said Romuald.

"And now that our business is done, I am off to Krakow to kill a certain sorceress who left me to rot in that tree."

Romuald was sticken with guilt at the thought of letting loose this horrible spirit. What evil was sure to come of it! Thinking quickly, he said, "What magic you possess! I am quite amazed. Can you show me that trick again?"

"What trick is that?" asked the faerie, puffing himself up proudly.

"The one where you fit inside that bottle. Seeing you now, I'd hardly dare believe you were once so small."

"It is not often I find one to share my talents with. Since you freed me, I will grant you this desire." And so the faerie man shrank down small, aye smaller than a toad, and crept back into the glass bottle.

As quick as summer lightning, Romuald picked up the stopper and jammed it into the hole. Then he took out his pen and painted three fresh crosses on the stopper. "In the name of the Holy Trinity, I bind you!" he shouted.

Mad with anger the spirit screeched at the trader, but it was of no use. He was stuck tight and stuck he would remain until someone else should chance to come by. And who knows when that will be? The mountains are high, the woods are dark and thick, and few are the travelers that stray from the path.

Romuald returned to the city, and found that the faerie spoke truth about the phials. The Water of Life healed the sick and the red liquid turned anything it touched to gold, and neither phial ran dry, no matter how often it was used.

The Water Snake

Every mythology has some form of the World Serpent, whether it be the snake in the Garden of Eden, the Midgard Worm of the Norse, or Koshchei the Deathless of the Russians. To the Poles he is sometimes called Waz. Snakes have long been regarded as symbols of everlasting life because of their ability to shed their skin, emerging "reborn." Later myth denotes the snake as the spirit of the hearth, once the center of birth and death in the home. A few tales of women marrying snakes survive.

It was springtime. The ice of the rivers had broken up and been swept away by the current. The young girls of the village, despite the lingering chill, went down to the river to bathe. They all stripped down to their shifts and waded into the water amidst squeals and giggles.

When they came out again, Emma found that a large, multi-colored snake had settled on her dress. "I told you to drape it across a branch," scoffed her sister. "How will you rid yourself of that creature?"

"Shoo!" Emma waved her hands before the snake's face. "Off with you now!" The other girls had dressed and were standing near Emma and the snake. "Shoo!" they all cried, waving sticks in the air.

The snake flicked its tongue in the air and said, "You can have your dress back, Emma, but only if you marry me."

"Marry? You? I don't think we'd suit each other at all!" Emma protested. "Just give me back my dress, will you?"

"Promise him anyway, and let's get home," said her sister. "How will he hold you to such a promise, anyway? Besides, you can't walk back through the village in your shift. Mother will surely scold you!"

"Say you'll marry him!" urged the other girls.

"Very well," sighed Emma. "I'll do it. I will be your bride." The snake slithered off her dress and without saying a word disappeared into the undergrowth.

Emma and her sister went home and very soon forgot about the whole incident.

Spring passed, and summer too, and one morning Emma walked into the front yard to see a great assembly of snakes twisting and slithering up to the porch. "What nonsense is this?" she cried. "Mother, Mother, come quick!"

Her mother came outside and looked at the company of snakes. "Foolish girl, what have you done? What magic have you meddled with?"

"I didn't know, Mother!" wailed the frightened girl. "I didn't know the snake would hold me to my promise of marriage!"

"Into the house, quickly!" snapped her mother, and dragged the girl inside. They lay the bolt across the door and said a quick prayer. Outside, they could hear the snakes throwing their bodies against the door.

"Emma, I told you not to make a promise to the snake!" screeched her sister. "Now look what's happened."

"Liar! You urged me to!" shouted Emma.

"Enough!" said their mother. "Onto the stove, now!"

The snakes rolled themselves into a great ball and rolled into the door, smashing it to kindling. Then they wound themselves around poor Emma's limbs and dragged her away, leaving her mother and her sister where they stood.

They dragged the girl down to the river's edge and pulled her beneath the surface of the water. For a long time her poor mother cried on the shore's edge, but her daughter never resurfaced.

Many years went by, and Emma lived beneath the waves with her snake husband. She had many children, each of whom she loved dearly. But she grew homesick. "Please, my dear, let me visit my mother. I have missed her all this time."

"I will take you to her," said her husband, and together they swam to the shore. "When you are ready to come home, call out to me, 'Waz, I am ready!' and I will fetch you."

So Emma went to her mother's cottage, her children in tow, and knocked on the door. "I am home, Mother!" she said when an old woman came to the door.

"You have done well, my daughter," said the old woman when she saw her daughter's costly garments and bejeweled hands. "And I see you have brought me grandchildren. Are you home to stay?"

"No. When our visit is done, I will return to the water's edge and call out, '*Waz*, I am ready!' Then my husband will fetch me."

"Ah, I see," said the old woman thoughtfully. "Why don't you and your children rest by the fire, and I will fetch us some cheese from the storehouse."

The old woman was still bitter that her daughter had been stolen from her. She went to the storehouse, but only long enough to grab her great axe, the one she used for chopping wood. Then she crept to the water's edge and said softly, "*Waz*, I am ready!" No sooner did the snake husband show himself than the old woman lifted her axe and whack! split his head in two. The river ran dark with his blood, and his lifeless body sank beneath the waves. "There," the old woman spat into the waves, "what's done is done and can't be undone."

"You've been gone a long while," said Emma when the old woman returned. "It is nearly time for me to go. But I promise we will visit again soon."

"If you must, Daughter, you must. It was good seeing you."

So Emma and her children went to the river's edge. She called out, "*Waz*, I am ready!" Then, "*Waz*, my husband, come fetch your wife and children!" And, "*Waz*, where are you? Can you not hear me? I wish to return home."

Poor Emma continued to call for her husband until one of her children tugged on her skirts. "Mama, Mama!" he said, "I see Father! He is sleeping in the reeds!" There, tangled in the growth, was the body of her dead husband.

"Ah me, she has killed him!" wailed Emma, and she fell to her knees.

The tears fell like rain on the lifeless body of her husband, sparkling like tiny jewels in the sun.

"Mama!" sang out one of her children. "Look, Mama! He's waking up!"

"I have been restored by the Water of Life," said the snake father. "Your tears have brought me back from the grave."

"It is time to go home, my husband," said Emma, embracing the snake most tenderly. "And never more shall we return to the village of my youth." They all returned to the watery kingdom, never to be seen again.

The *Poudnica*

The Poudnica *are whirlwinds which are sometimes also called, "Maidens of Midday." A* Poudnica *is usually seen on hot summer days as a whirling cloud of dust. In Polish folklore she is sometimes described as a crone who appears when the sun is at its highest, to drive people into heatstroke or to cut off their heads with a scythe. My grandmother called them Dust Devils.*

One brilliant morning in late summer, a farmer named Arek was working in his field alongside his brother Jozef. They paused to drink from their flasks, sitting in the shade beneath a rowan tree. "It is terribly hot today," complained Arek.

"I agree," said Jozef. "On a day like this I want nothing more than a cool swim in the river."

Just then there was a disturbance in the fields. A whirlwind came sweeping down the rows, knocking over the shocks of ripening grain. Before Jozef had time to think, Arek had already taken out his knife and thrown it into the middle of the dust cloud. Instantly it dispersed, but when the dust settled the farmer couldn't find his knife.

No matter how hard the two men searched, the knife was nowhere to be found. "It is not here," said Jozef, "perhaps we should just go home."

The brothers returned to Jozef's cottage where his wife was preparing the midday meal. She stood by the stove, her hand wrapped in a bandage.

"What is wrong, Izydora?" asked Jozef.

"It's nothing," she said. "I just cut myself peeling vegetables."

They all sat down to eat when Arek said, "May I borrow a knife? I lost mine in the fields." Before Izydora could stop him, he stood to get one from the chest. There he found his own knife.

"Where did you get this?" he asked quietly.

"From market," said the woman. "I bought it from a traveling tinker."

"I think your wife lies, Jozef," the man said to his brother. "For I once carved my own name into the handle of this knife. You can still see it. This is the knife I cast at the dust devil."

That is how they knew that Izydora was a *Poudnica*, a whirlwind witch.

The Doctor

The following is an urban legend, a modern Polish folktale with an "alien" theme. Various versions of this story include some that stretch back to the early 1900s.

At the end of World War II, a meteor shower could be seen from all villages along the Tatras. For many nights it looked as if the very stars were falling from the sky. It was not long afterwards that a strange disease swept through the mountains. No one was safe. Men, women and children all fell victim to the disfiguring illness, and no doctor could cure it.

The people fell to praying, as there was little else they could do. A bright light appeared in the heavens, brighter than any star, and from the direction of the light came a young doctor. He was quite unlike any of the people who lived in the mountain villages. He was very tall and very thin, with large luminescent eyes and white hair. "I have a tincture for you," he said. "It will cure this disease and no more of your children will die from it."

No one questioned the stranger. They had tried everything else, and would try this, too.

It was a miracle! As soon as the medicine was given to the sick they were cured. When the elders went in search of the doctor, to thank him for what he had done, he was nowhere to be found. To this day the people along the Tatras wonder about their strange visitor and the meteor shower that heralded his arrival.

The Unfinished Tune

The trumpet, whether made of wood, cane, bark, bone or metal, has been used since Neolithic times for both magical and practical reasons. According to Funk and Wagnall's Folklore Dictionary, *trumpets have heralded burial rites, initiation ceremonies, healing spells, expulsion of evil spirits, contacting the dead, communication with the gods, and have sounded military signals and general alarms. Before the widespread use of telephone and radio, a trumpet was used to send signals across great distances. It should not be surprising, then, that the great city of Krakow has its own trumpeter legend.*

What is that music floating on the breeze? Is it the organist of the tiny church down the road practicing for Sunday service? Or is it the angels in heaven sounding out hosannas from on high? The strange music fills the streets of Krakow, and just as suddenly as it begins, it stops — cut off in mid-note.

Ask any citizen of Krakow about the tune, and they will tell you it is the *Hejnal*, played from the tower of the Kosciol Mariacki, the Church of Saint Mary, every hour on the hour. It commemorates the death of a trumpeter who fulfilled his duty to Poland at the cost of his own life.

Many centuries ago, in the dark days of the Middle Ages, the Tartar army was on the march. Many great and powerful cities had already fallen to the advancing troops. Even Kiev, which was thought to be well-defended, could not protect herself.

The Tartars were a fearsome force, sparing no one in their path. Refugees from the countryside poured through Krakow's gates, praying to the Lord that the army would pass by the city.

But the Tartars came. One dark night they fell upon the outlying villages like a pack of dogs, pillaging and burning everything in their path. They cut a wide swath of destruction through the Polish countryside. But as dawn rose, the citizens of Krakow could see that one church still remained standing, the Kosciol Mariacki, the Church of Saint Mary.

The trumpeter of the Kosciol Mariacki had watched from his tower window and saw the army advancing on the city. Like many trumpeters before him, he had sworn that he would always sound the *Hejnal*, the hymn to Our Lady, even in the face of death. With a strange joy in his heart, he lifted the trumpet to his lips and sounded the hymn, "For Poland!" he thought. But before he had the chance to finish, a Tartar archer pierced his throat with an arrow. The tune was cut off mid-note, but it was enough to remind the Polish people that they were fighting for God as well as country.

The Church of St. Mary no longer stands out alone in the fields surrounding the city, but has been closed in by other buildings. Only the tower and the trumpeter who stands in the window can be seen from any distance.

For generations, the trumpeters of Krakow have sworn to protect the city. Now, every hour of every day, they play the *Hejnal* from the tower as a tribute to the ancient hero. The music always stops at the same moment when the brave trumpeter was killed.

Tune in to the radio and you will hear the *Hejnal* played over the airwaves, an enduring symbol of Polish pride and independence.

Oath of the Krakow Trumpeters

"I swear to the Almighty Lord God that I will be obedient to the gentlemen of the Krakovian Council, and faithful to the entire city in the service which I render with the trumpet.

"I will be diligent in keeping watch and sound the alarm of fire whenever and wherever it appears, in the city or behind it.

"I will sound upon the trumpet the hours of the night and day, and without the permission of his honor the burgomaster.

"I will sound the trumpet at no man's request,...and all this observe which belongs to my duties, so help me God."

— From *The Book of Oaths*, Krakow, Poland, 1671

Bibliography and Recommended Reading

- Bain, R.N. *Cossack Fairy and Folktales.* New York: A.L. Burst, 1890.
- Bruce, Marjory. *A Treasury of Tales.* New York: Thomas Y. Crowell Co., 1927.
- Byrde, Elsie. *The Polish Fairy Book.* New York: Frederick A. Stoke Co., 1925.
- Chrypinski, Anna, editor. *Polish Customs.* Detroit: Friends of Polish Art, 1977.
- Curtain, Jeremiah. *Myths and Folktales of the Russians, Slavs and Magyars.* Boston: Little, Brown & Co., 1890.
- Gaster, Moses. *Bird and Beast Stories.* London: Sidgwick & Jackson, Ltd., 1915.
- Glinski, A.J. *Polish Fairy Tales.* London: John Lane Co., 1920.
- Gimbutas, Marijas. *The Goddesses and Gods of Old Europe.* Los Angeles: University of California Press, 1992.
- Groom, Francis Hindes. *Gypsy Folk Tales.* London: Hurst & Blackert, Ltd., 1899.
- Ivanits, Linda J. *Russian Folk Beliefs.* New York: M.E. Sharpe, Inc., 1989.
- Jones, Prudence, and Nigel Pennick. *A History of Pagan Europe.* New York: Rutledge, 1997.
- Knab, Sophie Hodorowicz. *Polish Customs, Traditions, & Folklore.* New York: Hippocrene Books, 1993.
- Knab, Sophie Hodorowicz. *Polish Herbs, Flowers, and Folk Medicine.* New York: Hippocrene Books, 1995.
- Kuhn, A. *Norddeutsche Sagen, Marchen und Geshichte.* Leipzig: F.A. Brockhaus, 1848.
- Kulikowski, Mark. *A Bibliography of Slavic Mythology.* Columbus, Ohio: Slavica Publishers, 1989.
- Lang, Andrew. *The Yellow Fairy Book.* New York, Toronto, London, Sydney: McGraw Hill Book Co., 1894.
- Lemnis, Maria, and Henryk Vitry. *Old Polish Traditions in the Kitchen.* New York: Hippocrene Books, 1998.
- Steele, Robert. *The Garland of Fairy Tales.* New York: R.M. McBride & Co., 1916.
- Waldherr, Kris. *The Book of Goddesses.* Hillsboro, Oregon: Beyond Words Publishing, Inc., 1995.
- Wratislaw, A.H. *Sixty Folktales from Slavonic Sources.* Boston: Houghton-Mifflin, 1890.

Made in the USA
Monee, IL
16 March 2023

29984224R00066